InVerse 2021

Italian Poets in Translation

Edited by
Brunella Antomarini
Berenice Cocciolillo
Rosa Filardi

JOHN CABOT UNIVERSITY PRESS

Published by John Cabot University Press
www.johncabot.edu

Copublished by The Rowman & Littlefield Publishing Group, Inc.
4501 Forbes Boulevard, Suite 200, Lanham, Maryland 20706
www.rowman.com

6 Tinworth Street, London SE11 5AL, United Kingdom

Copyright © 2021 by John Cabot University Press

Via della Lungara 233, Roma 00165
© Copyright of unpublished works held by the individual poets

All rights reserved. No part of this book may be reproduced in any form or by any electronic or mechanical means, including information storage and retrieval systems, without written permission from the publisher, except by a reviewer who may quote passages in a review.

In loving memory of John Cabot University Head Librarian Elisabetta Morani, whose passion for books and learning continues to inspire us.

CONTENTS

- 5   **INTRODUCTION**
- 7   **TRANSLATORS**
- 8   **CREDITS**

- 13   **GIOVANNA CRISTINA VIVINETTO**
- 25   **RENATA MORRESI**
- 37   **TIZIANO SCARPA**
- 49   **VINCENZO BAGNOLI**
- 61   **CHANDRA LIVIA CANDIANI**
- 73   **BEPPE SEBASTE**
- 87   **NEFELI MISURACA**
- 99   **CARLO BOASSA**
- 111   **FABIO ORECCHINI**
- 123   **FRANCA MANCINELLI**
- 133   **FABIO DONALISIO**
- 157   **GINEVRA LILLI**
- 169   **GIANNI D'ELIA**
- 181   **CESARE VIVIANI**
- 193   **FABRIZIO SANI**
- 205   **DONATELLA DELLA RATTA**
- 219   **JONIDA PRIFTI**

- 233   **BIOGRAPHIES**

INTRODUCTION

The challenges caused by the COVID-19 pandemic have led to a delay in the release of this volume of our anthology. But in very difficult times we are reminded of the importance of keeping the dialogue between different languages alive by providing readers all over the world with opportunities to listen to the voices of poets. We are encouraged by the ever-growing interest in *InVerse* and are committed to renewing it every few years. It is heartening to see the unique work of so many talented young poets. Interestingly, it seems that the more global and complex societies become, the more young writers feel the need to render the experience of this complexity in verse, that is, in a way that requires a paradigm shift in comprehension.

The *InVerse* festival continues to be a celebration of the joyous ritual of verse, making poetry as much as possible a popular event that overcomes the limits of its niche reception and makes it available to a wide audience.

Since *InVerse* was born as a festival and an anthology of poetry in translation, we continue to take great pride in supporting the art of translation. In an age when translators are often asked to work quickly and mechanically to satisfy publishers' needs to distribute instant books, we hold on to the idea that a translator has an enormous personal responsibility in reconstructing a poem. When this demanding work is done well, it must be recognized, in poet Osip Mandel'štam's words, "as an event and an honor for the author and a feast for the reader; a translation that does not come from the translator's inner need may cause huge damages in the unconscious laboratory of language."

Brunella Antomarini   Berenice Cocciolillo   Rosa Filardi

TRANSLATORS

Vincenzo Bagnoli: ALLISON GRIMALDI DONAHUE

Carlo Boassa: GABRIELE POOLE

Chandra Livia Candiani: BERENICE COCCIOLILLO

Gianni D'Elia: JENNIFER PANEK

Donatella Della Ratta: KAY WALLACE

Fabio Donalisio: LAUREN SUNSTEIN

Ginevra Lilli: RICCARDO PUGLIESE

Franca Mancinelli: ANDREW RUTT and ELENA BUIA RUTT

Nefeli Misuraca: NEFELI MISURACA

Renata Morresi: GABRIELE POOLE

Fabio Orecchini: ALLISON GRIMALDI DONAHUE

Jonida Prifti: JAMES SCHWARTEN

Fabrizio Sani: ANDREA CASSON

Tiziano Scarpa: BERENICE COCCIOLILLO

Beppe Sebaste: TOM BAILEY

Cesare Viviani: JAMES SCHWARTEN

Giovanna Cristina Vivinetto: SEAN MARK

CREDITS

The poems in this collection are unpublished, with the exception of these poems, previously published in:

Vincenzo Bagnoli: "Violetta," from *Teenage Suicide, Soundscapes. 33 Giri Extended Play*, Messina, Carteggi Letterari, 2018; also appeared in the music album *Bologna '67-77* (New Model Label, 2012) by The Stratten.

Chandra Livia Candiani: the first, second and third poems are from *La bambina pugile*, Turin: Einaudi 2014. The last two are from *Fatti vivo*, Turin: Einaudi, 2017.

Franca Mancinelli: some fragments of the sequence in this volume have appeared, in a different version, under the title *Verso una zona più limpida dello sguardo* in "L'Ulisse" *Poetiche per il XXI secolo*, no. 18, 2015.

Nefeli Misuraca: the first, second, and fourth poems are from *La Solitudine maestosa*, Milan: La Vita Felice, 2017.

Renata Morresi: poems from "Di fragile costituzione," in *Terzo Paesaggio*, Milan: Aragno 2019. In 2017 they appeared in Spanish in *Italia, Poesía: Presente. Antología de poesía italiana contemporánea* (Huerga & Fierro Editores, Madrid, 2017, tr. R. Buffi).

Fabio Orecchini: "Per Os" (Sigismundus Editrice, San Benedetto del Tronto, 2016); "Figura" (Oèdipus Edizioni, collana CromaK, Salerno, 2019) is a study from Euripides' *Alcestis*.

Jonida Prifti: "Oriane" acrostic-art book (HD Edizioni, Rome, 2017), "Liri SM" (Canti Magnetici, 2019).

Fabrizio Sani: "Naupatia" appeared in *Si innamoravano tutti di me e io del loro amore*, Turin: SuiGeneris, 2018.

Tiziano Scarpa: *Le nuvole e i soldi*, Turin: Einaudi, 2018.

Beppe Sebaste: *Come un cinghiale in una macchia d'inchiostro*, Turin: Nino Aragno, 2018. The text of "The O of Earth" was modified by the author, with the addition of verses.

Cesare Viviani: *La forma della vita*, Turin: Einaudi 2005.

Giovanna Cristina Vivinetto: *Dolore minimo*, Novara: Interlinea 2018.

InVerse 2021

GIOVANNA CRISTINA VIVINETTO

La prima perdita furono le mani.
Mi lasciò il tocco ingenuo
che si addentrava nelle cose, le scopriva
con piglio bambino – le plasmava.
Erano mani che non sapevano
ritrarsi: mani di dodici anni,
mani di figli che tendono al cono
di luce – che non sanno ancora
giungersi in preghiera.
Mani profonde – come laghi
in cui nessuno verrebbe a cercare,
mani silenti come vecchi scrigni
chiusi – mani inviolate.

La prima scoperta furono le mani.
Ricevetti un tocco adulto che sa
esattamente dove posarsi – mani
ampie e concave di una madre
che si accosta alla soglia ad aspettare;
mani di legno e di fiori
di ciliegio – mani che rinascono.
Mani che sanno aggrapparsi anche
all'esatta consistenza del nulla.

Hands were the first thing I lost.
Gone was the innocent touch
that probed things, uncovered them
with childlike pluck – and moulded them.
They were hands that did not know
retreat: twelve-year-old's hands,
that children stretch to reach the cone
of light – hands still unsure how to
join in prayer.
Hands deep – like lakes
where no one would look,
hands silent like old, closed
treasure chests – hands unbreached.

Hands were the first thing I found.
I was given an adult touch
that knows exactly where to rest –
broad, concave hands of a mother
who waits at the doorstep; hands
made of wood and cherry blossom –
hands that are born again.
Hands that know even how to grip
the exact texture of nothingness.

La seconda perdita fu la luce.
La malattia mi tolse la vista
dei campi abbacinati dal sole,
la trama arsa e viva dei litorali
siciliani dei miei tredici anni.
Passai quegli anni tra i fili
di panni stesi divorati dal sole,
vasi sbriciolati di terracotta
dove steli di basilico e lavanda
si inerpicavano verso la linea
del cielo – quasi a raggiungerla,
a toccarla. La luce era tutto.

La seconda scoperta fu la luce.
Non la luce che accende i terrazzi
né quella che assottiglia le strisce
di costa, ma la luce delle case
al tramonto – che si mischia all'ombra,
la luce setacciata dall'intreccio
dei rami e quella che si schiarisce
a fatica dopo un temporale
– dopo un grave malanno.
Conquistai la luce intatta dei corpi
vergini – delle fonti d'acqua
perenni che nessuno sa.

Light was the second thing I lost.
Illness took from me the sight
of fields dazzled by the sun,
the outline of the Sicilian coast,
parched and alive, of my thirteenth year.
I spent those years between the rows
of hung laundry devoured by the sun,
crumbled terracotta vases
where stems of lavender and basil
clambered towards the line
of sky – to reach and almost
touch it. Light was all there was.

Light was the second thing I found.
Not the light that ignites balconies
or thins out the strips of coast,
but the light of houses
at sunset – that mixes with shadow,
the light sifted by the knots
of branches, the light that struggles
to brighten after a storm
– or serious sickness.
I took for me the intact light
of virgin bodies – of endless
springs that no one knows.

La terza perdita fu il perdono.
Avrei voluto scusarmi per i toni
accesi verso il tuo non comprendere,
la rara gentilezza dei miei
quattordici anni quando parlavi
senza premesse. Ma la colpa
non era di nessuno: non era tua
che mi indicavi il corpo e mi dicevi
di stare attenta, che non sarebbe stato
facile – non era mia che non riuscivo
a perdonare il tuo insinuarti
maternamente tra pelle e nervi
a scovare tutte le incertezze, gli stalli
che a quel tempo non avevo.

La terza scoperta fu il perdono.
Quando fui grande abbastanza
per capire cosa volesse dire
essere madre, un perdono tondo
e commosso provai per te, e provai
per le altre donne-bambine come me
e lo provai per me, che tenevo
fino a quel punto il filo rosso dell'infanzia
e da un giorno all'altro, adultamente,
non tenevo più.

Forgiveness was the third thing I lost.
I would've liked to say sorry for my angry
response to your nonunderstanding,
the rare kindness of my fourteenth year
when you spoke your mind. But the blame
lay with no one: not with you
who'd show me my body and say
be careful, this wasn't going to be
easy – nor with me, who couldn't
forgive your maternal prying
between skin and nerve
to unearth all uncertainties,
the qualms I didn't have back then.

Forgiveness was the third thing I found.
When I was old enough
to understand what being
a mother meant, I felt for you forgiveness
moved and whole, felt it
for other child-women like me,
felt it for myself, who had held
the thread of childhood until then
and, adultly, from one day to the next,
I no longer did.

Per anni ho provato a stanarti
dal doppiofondo umido delle mie
ossa. Sarebbe stato uno spremerti
via dagli occhi se solo ti avessi
trovata in tempo – invece è stato
un chiedere invano senza risposta.

Sarà che certe cose a quindici anni
non si possono ancora capire
– mentre tu in silenzio già strisciavi
nelle stanze disabitate
incorrotte del mio corpo.
Sarà che la voce interna fiorisce
solo a forza di strappi e toppe
mal ricucite – da lì sguscia l'anima.

Eppure seppellito sotto mucchi
di foglie secche un indizio c'era
– un debole presupposto
inavvertitamente esisteva:
il rifiuto del padre, il rigetto
della sua assenza – la sua voragine,
la preponderanza del ruolo
materno – l'ombra femminile
troppo a lungo riflessa.

Fu nel vuoto che ti conficcasti:
una scheggia di legno mentre
si chiudono le finestre
che sbattono sole al vento.
Fosti il compromesso da accettare,
la voce interna da nutrire,
la preghiera da salmodiare
in ginocchio. L'ultima toppa
sgraziata da ricucire – sul cuore.

For years I tried to drive you out
from the damp false bottom
of my bones. It would've meant
squeezing you out of my eyes
if only I'd found you in time – instead
it was asking in vain with no response.

Perhaps at fifteen certain things
can't be understood yet
– while already you slithered
silently in my body's empty
and uncorrupted rooms.
Perhaps the inner voice
blooms only with the rips
and poorly-sewn patches
– from which the soul slips out.

And yet buried under heaps
of dry leaves was a clue
– a feeble premise did
inadvertently exist:
refusal of the father, rejection
of his absence – his chasm,
predominance of the maternal
role – the feminine shadow
too long reflected.

It was in the void that you were lodged:
a wooden splinter as windows are closed
that beat alone in the wind.
You were the compromise to swallow,
the inner voice to feed,
the bent-knee prayer to psalmodize.
The last clumsy patch –
to sew back on my heart.

Una volta l'anno discendevo
a te, madre, d'autunno.
Tu mi accoglievi con foglie
tra le mani che disperdevi
al vento ad ogni mio arrivo.
Capivi, madre, l'ordine nascosto
delle cose – così quando ai miei otto
anni sussurravi "figlia mia",
io ti rinnegavo tante volte
quante erano le foglie che svolavi.
"Siamo foglie d'autunno, figlia mia"
era il tuo unico, dolce monito.

Per i successivi dieci anni
discesi a te ogni autunno, madre
e ti vedevo, com'eri solita fare,
disperdere foglie e sibilare
tra le labbra nomi di donna
– nomi di figlia a me ignoti.

L'autunno dell'undicesimo anno
scesi a te, madre, ma non ti trovai più:
le foglie restavano ammucchiate
– non c'erano mani a liberarle nel vento.
Ti chiamai, sussurrai il tuo nome,
sciogliendo la verità in esso nascosta.

Quell'autunno al posto tuo,
invece delle tue mani dispersi
le foglie, mi nominai al vento,
riemersi dall'inferno che mi moriva
in petto: fu così che mi arresi
al dolore dei nomi quando capii
che quel nome che andavi chiamando
era il mio, madre.

Once a year I'd go down
to you, mother, in autumn.
You welcomed me with leaves
in your hands you'd scatter
in the wind each time I arrived.
You understood, mother, the hidden
order of things – so when I was eight
and you'd whisper "daughter,"
I'd deny you once for each leaf you cast.
"My daughter, we are autumn leaves"
your sole, sweet warning.

For the next ten years
I went down to you, mother, each autumn
and saw you scatter leaves,
as you used to, and hiss
between your lips names of women
– daughter's names I didn't know.

The autumn of the eleventh year
I went down to you, mother, but could find you no more:
the leaves were in a heap
– there were no hands to free them in the wind.
I called you, whispered your name,
untangling the truth hidden therein.

That autumn in your place
instead of your hands I scattered
the leaves, named myself to the wind,
climbed out of the hell dying
in my chest: and thus I yielded
to the pain of names when I realized
the name you'd been calling, mother,
was mine.

RENATA MORRESI

Deve esserci un nome per la condizione depressiva che colpisce chi è precario o in cerca di occupazione. Si è, in realtà, molto occupati, oppressi da uno squatting continuo. Nel corso degli anni le forme dell'organizzazione collettiva, della rivendicazione, del reclamare voce si sono sempre più assottigliate, e 'resistere' è sembrato diventare una faccenda personale. Io mi rifugiavo spesso nel sonno. Le citazioni tra virgolette sono tratte dalla Costituzione italiana.

Vive dalle nove, nove e un quarto.
Rimane a letto. Il letto è in possesso
del tempo, come la nazione. Carta
bianca, cartina distesa, catena
montuosa, ne è la solitaria
presidente. Signora,
Signore, Buongiorno, Un
Inno. Canta. Presente
senza ombre. Atto verbale.
Angelo. Fatto di scrivere.
Le formalità sono piene.

There must be a name for that depressive condition affecting those who do not have a stable job or are unemployed. In reality they are very occupied, oppressed by a continuous squatting. Over the years, the modes of collective organization, of political struggle, of demanding to be heard have become increasingly rare and 'resisting' seemed to have become a personal matter. I often took refuge in sleep. The citations in quotes are from the Italian Constitution.

She lives from nine, nine fifteen.
She stays in bed. The bed is the owner
of time, like the nation. Carte
blanche, open map, mountain
range, she is its solitary
president. Ma'am,
Sir, Good Morning, a
Hymn. Sings. Present
without shadows cast. Verbal act.
Angel. Made of writing.
The formalities are full.

Se esce dispone gli occhi da un lato come lenti
in modo che gli altri la vedano guardare da una parte
che non è loro ma è ammessa, che non è parte
cosciente di chi è intorno ma resta nell'unità,
sovrappensiero. Rotando le pupille nel raggio
esteso o stretto dell'orizzonte necessario,
si finge reale per rimanere reale, ovvero fuori
("sia come singolo, sia nelle formazioni sociali")
la stessa patria, la stessa casa, lo stesso crac.

If she goes out, she arranges her eyes to the side like lens
so that others may see her looking towards one side
that is not theirs but is allowed, that is not a conscious
part of those who are around but remains within the unity,
absentmindedly. Rotating her pupils in the extended
or restricted radius of the necessary horizon,
she pretends to be real to remain real, that is outside
("both as individual, and in social bodies")
the same motherland, the same house, the same ruin.

Finge di liberare il viso dai capelli invece li aggiunge
e se qualcuno la intercetta con lo sguardo
affonda nella tasca del giubbotto e tasta
la cosa che ha lasciato maturare,
la cosa che fa clac tra le sue dita,
la cosa dell'attenzione completa,
che non mangia più, cosa avanzata, avanza
oh dolce onnivora Spinoza, cosa
incomprensibile dalla differenziata, la cosa ultra-
formata, con parti in plastica, metallo, carta, vegetale,
chi non la teme?
Dovrebbe riuscire a entrare in auto
prima che la vedano.

She pretends to brush her hair from her eyes and instead adds more
and if someone intercepts her gaze
she dives inside the pocket of her jacket and gropes
the thing she has allowed to mature,
the thing that goes clack between her fingers
the thing of total attention,
that she no longer eats, the leftover thing, left
oh sweet omnivorous Spinoza, incomprehensible
thing from separate collection, the ultra-
formed thing, with parts of plastic, metal, paper, vegetable,
who does not fear it?
She should be able to get inside the car
before they see her.

Studia l'inconscio del curriculum
come se il lavoro fosse un fatto psicologico.
Sforzo inane: non si libera
di una frase, un'officina
e altre cose che la abitano
da sera a mattina, quel giro di blues.
Ci prova. Ricomporle tutte, le code sparse,
sperma di materie, alla stessa dispersione.
Dimenticarle tutte e nei particolari,
una frase che torna – "il diritto",
"effettivo", "al progresso" –
un'officina alla volta, una cosa in se stessa,
e quel classico giro
dov'è l'errore, dov'è il merito.
(La disfunzione è un lavoro a tempo pieno)

She studies the unconscious of the résumé
as if working were a psychological thing.
Vain attempt: you can't get rid
of a phrase a workshop,
and of other things that inhabit her
from night to morning, that blues riff.
She tries. Putting them all together, the bits and ends,
sperm of matter, to the same dispersion.
Forget them all and in detail,
a phrase that recurs – "the right,"
"effective," "to the progress" --
one workshop at a time, one thing in itself,
and that classic round
where's the error, where the merit.
(Dysfunction is a full time job)

Al risveglio trova un sole
che sta entrando nel sole.
Un nome pronunciato
Da più secoli fa eco
normale, acufene.
Sul boschetto di pini
sta un affresco di pini
piegati dal vento.
In quel punto
è reale il simbolico
albero, scoperto
al levante,
fragile, fa male
anche solo a guardarlo
nocchiuto, deforme.
Difficile proteggerlo
se tu stessa sei un albero.
Li tocca per pensare
che non siano colore
l'un l'altro.

Upon waking up she finds a sun
that is entering the sun.
A name pronounced
For many centuries echoes
normally, tinnitus.
Over the pine grove
hovers a fresco of pines
bent by the wind.
In that place
the symbolic tree
is real, exposed
to the east wind,
fragile, it hurts
even to look at it,
gnarled, deformed.
Hard to protect it
if you yourself are a tree.
She touches them to think
that they are not color
for each other.

TIZIANO SCARPA

Certe volte che non sono morto #1

nel millenovecentosettantuno
inseguo stefano gli corro dietro
fra il calcetto e il tavolo da ping pong
ridiamo tutti e due
senza voltarsi lui dietro la schiena
fa come un colpo d'ali
con tutte e due le braccia
spinge forte la porta alle sue spalle

i battenti massicci a tutta forza
mi sbattono contemporaneamente
su tutte e due le tempie

mentre deliro a casa sul divano
in piena commozione cerebrale
mia madre fa di tutto
per spiegare alla morte
che in sala giochi dei chierichetti non vale

Some Times That I Did Not Die #1

in nineteen seventy-one
I chase stefano I run after him
between the foosball and the ping pong table
we both laugh
without turning around,
he slams the door behind him
with both arms, as if beating wings

the massive shutters
simultaneously slam me
on both temples in full force

while I'm delirious at home on the couch
in the midst of a cerebral concussion
my mother does all she can
to explain to death
that in the altar boys' game room, it doesn't count

Certe volte che non sono morto #3

la notte che volevo suicidarmi
ma seriamente, prima dell'esame
di storia medievale
mi ero ridotto all'ultimo momento
sfogliavo il manuale
sei secoli in sei ore, era un esame
obbligatorio nel piano di studi
per poter fare un giorno il professore
non mi importava un cazzo
di fare il professore
io mi ero iscritto a lettere
per sprofondare dentro la scrittura
stare vicino ai morti
alle loro parole
(cosa che quella notte
non mi riuscì per poco)
riuscivo ad imparare solo quello
che faceva parte della mia anima
(voglio dire che all'università
scoprii nuove parti della mia anima
di nome austin tesauro bachtin frazer
savinio chomsky eccetera)
ma quella notte fra innocenzo terzo
e la crociata contro gli albigesi
cercai in tutta la stanza una lametta
era il ventidue luglio
milleduecentonove
massacro di béziers

Some Times That I Did Not Die #3

the night I wanted to kill myself
but seriously, before the
medieval history exam
I had waited until the last minute
I leafed through the textbook
six centuries in six hours, it was a
requirement for my major
so that I could one day be a professor
I did not give a shit
about being a professor
I was studying literature
just to sink into writing
to be close to the dead
and their words
(and on that night
I almost managed to)
I could only learn what
was part of my soul
(I mean at university
I discovered new parts of my soul
named austin bachtin frazer
savinio chomsky etcetera)
but that night between innocent III
and the crusade against the albigensians
I looked all over the room for a razor blade
it was the twenty-second of July
twelve hundred nine
the massacre at béziers

Mia madre

Se esisto è grazie a lei, è colpa sua.
Perciò mia madre avrà
sempre ragione-torto
contemporaneamente.
È la mia insofferenza.
Io sono il suo creditore insolvente,
l'esoso debitore.

My Mother

If I exist it's thanks to her, it's her fault.
That's why my mother will always
be right – wrong
at the same time.
She's my intolerance.
I am her insolvent creditor,
her greedy debtor.

Esercizio di comprensione del testo #2

Ricopia la poesia
mettendo i versi in fila
senza andare a capo. Prova a rileggerla.
Che effetto fa in quella forma? È lo stesso
esprimersi senza intoppi rispetto
a un discorso che dice le sue cose
con quella specie di strano singhiozzo
che va a capo, ostinato, sempre a capo
come se il poeta avesse inghiottito
qualcosa che gli è andato di traverso?

E che cosa, secondo te, ha inghiottito?
Un rospo? Un animale macellato
e arrostito alla griglia
per cui sente pietà
e di cui allo stesso tempo è goloso?
È il singhiozzo di un ghiotto
quello che questi versi ti comunicano
con il loro andamento frammentato
sotto la crosta dei significati?
Il sottofondo del senso di colpa
non lo abbandona mai?
È questo che frattura
il ritmo dei suoi accenti?

Reading Comprehension Exercise #2

Copy the poem
one verse after another
without starting a new line. Try to reread it.
What's it like that way? Is it the same
to express it without snags, instead of
a discourse that talks
with that strange kind of hiccup
that starts a new line, stubborn, again and again
as if the poet had swallowed
something that went down the wrong way?

And what do you think he swallowed?
A toad? An animal slaughtered
and roasted on a grill
for whom he feels mercy
while at the same time craving?
Is it the hiccup of a glutton
that which these verses communicate
with their fragmented gait
under the crust of meanings?
Doesn't the backdrop of guilt
ever abandon him?
Is this what breaks
the rhythm of his accents?

Poesia scritta dalle parole #1

Siamo le parole.
Conteniamo i desideri dei morti,
le esperienze di chi non è ancora nato.
(contenere, v. tr.
1. tenere dentro di sé; 2. trattenere)

In questo istante siamo attraversate
da una mente, la tua.
Siamo un'intimità esteriore,
siamo escluse dentro di te.

Vorremmo poter spiare
che cosa ti stiamo facendo immaginare.
(ti stiamo facendo immaginare
noi che ti spiamo dall'interno)

Nessuno al mondo ti guarda così.

Poem Written by Words #1

We are the words.
We contain the desires of the dead,
the experiences of those not yet born.
(contain, transitive verb,
1. to hold within oneself; 2. to keep)

In this instant we are crossed
by a mind, yours.
We are an external intimacy,
we are excluded inside you.

We would like to spy
on what we are making you imagine.
(we are making you imagine
us spying on you from the inside)

No one on earth looks at you like this.

VINCENZO BAGNOLI

Zero (le mat)

Ormai non manca molto dice guarda la piega sempre più amara del labbro
la strada con l'asfalto rovinato e sono proprio i giorni di pioggia
di quel che il tempo lava via che restano incrostati in fondo al tempo

Guarda dice che sono sempre accese le luci dei lampioni e dei bar
anche nell'ora più buia e più tarda e guarda che la gente è per le strade
non c'è una notte fonda in cui sparire lanciando un ultimo urlo di rabbia

Dove sei dove sono dove andrò quanto lontani ancora saremo
l'eclissi del sabato sera e insieme tutte le altre figure dell'altrove
che resteranno sempre agli estremi confini del mondo in qualche attesa

Zero (le mat)

By now it won't be long she says look at the lip's fold get more and more bitter
the street with ruined asphalt and it's precisely the rainy days,
the sort of season that weather washes away, that are left encrusted at the end of time

Look he says the lights in the street lamps and cafes are always turned on
even at the darkest and latest hour and look at the people in the streets
there is no deep night in which to vanish letting out a final cry of anger

Where are you where am I where will I go how much longer will we be
the eclipse of Saturday night and together with all of the other figures from beyond
that are always there at the very edges of the earth, awaiting

Sketches for Dawn (Boote nel cielo boreale)

Hai messo proprio tutti i respiri sul freddo e piatto acciaio del sonno
e la ferrea gabbia del torace
ora è la sponda di un fiume invernale su cui non s'incontra mai nessuno.

Di tutto quanto non detto e non fatto resta la schiuma sui bordi dell'alba
la forza che ti manca nel mattino
il colore stonato dell'assenza, l'ombra del sogno nei raggi del sole.

Questo per sempre non avrà mai fine.

Non ha un principio, se non un chiarore di alba sfinita sotto una pioggia
di giorni e giorni, di tutta la notte
vuoto che dura fin dentro ai corpi come un pallido sole d'autunno.

Null'altro può durare come questo
un altro sguardo da oltre l'azzurro che scava dentro distanza e mancanza

Sketches for Dawn (Boötes in the northern light sky)

You put all of the breaths on the cold and flat steel of sleep
and the iron cage of the chest
now it is the shore of a winter river upon which you never meet anyone.

Of everything unsaid and not done there is a foam on the edges of dawn
the strength that you lack in the morning
the clashing color of absence, the shadow of a dream in the sun's rays.

This will be forever endless.

It has no beginning, if not a dim light of sunrise quashed under the rain
for days and days, and for the entire night
emptiness that lasts even inside bodies like a pale autumn sun.

Nothing else can last like this
another look from beyond the blue that digs into distance and loss

X lama   (24 hours)

Ancora un giorno infame come gli altri di eternit di ruggine e carbone
di polvere e fuliggine di ghisa di limatura di ferro e di asfalto.
Dicembre volta l'angolo in fretta e l'anno nuovo ci salta alla gola:
la quieta maestà del clima freddo è rotta dalla rabbia dell'industria.
Le nude travature del commercio, le crude verità del capitale
le trovi al tatto, in fondo alla notte, le ore più buie che durano a lungo.
E poi la morte bianca del risveglio nel grigio della cenere del tempo,
e del futuro andato già in fumo in tutte queste fabbriche del nulla,
fame meccanica che scava dentro le nostre budella l'annientamento.
E in questa nebbia gotica la storia è un incubo davvero senza fine
mentre nuotiamo nel mare di stelle della galassia perdendo nel vuoto
per sempre tutti gli atomi leggeri scomparsi in fondo agli angoli del cielo
nel vuoto del big rip, dell'entropia

X lama   (24 hours)

Still one infamous day like the others in eternit of rust and coal
of dust and cast iron soot of iron filings and of asphalt.
December turns the corner in a hurry and the new year jumps down our throat:
the quiet majesty of the cold climate is broken by the rage of industry.
The naked trusses of commerce, the crude truths of capital
you find them by touch, deep in the night, the darkest hours that last so long.
And the white death of awakening in the gray ash of time,
and the future already gone up in smoke in all of these factories of nothing,
mechanical hunger that digs annihilation within our bowels.
And in this gothic fog history is a nightmare truly without end
while we swim in the starry sea of the galaxy losing in the void
forever all the airy atoms vanished behind the corners of the sky
in the void of the big rip, of entropy

Lui comme sa bastille

Hai mai sentito un camion scaricare
macerie di una casa demolita
mattoni soprattutto laterizi
vetri infranti e piastrelle spezzate?
è un urlo stridulo e non un rombo
un'epica catastrofe sonora
ma solo frana di rottami sparsi.
Mixala ai Crystal Castles alla voce
di Alice Glass e alle distorsioni
di William Reid al suo muro del suono
se vuoi sapere come siamo fatti
sotto alla solita giacca di pelle
contro i muri bagnati di pioggia
in strade solitarie sull'asfalto
distrutto e sgretolato qui nel freddo

(2 dicembre 2014)

Lui comme sa bastille

Have you ever heard a truck unload
debris from a demolished house
bricks mostly of clay
shattered glass and cracked tiles?
it is a shrill cry and not a rumble
an epic sonic catastrophe
but only the collapse of random scraps.
Mix it with Crystal Castles with the voice
of Alice Glass and the distortions
of William Reid with his wall of sound
if you want to know what we are made of
under the usual leather jacket
against walls wet with rain
in lonely streets on the asphalt
wrecked and devastated here in the cold

(December 2, 2014)

Violetta

Violetta,
Metti in rilievo che è proprio la fretta
Il vero guaio dei nervi dolenti
poi basta prendersi in farmacia
qualche analgesico o aspirina
L'ispirazione © è una pratica lenta
un esercizio di respirazione

rit. «vorrei avere una lapide di marmo
e invece è polistirolo espanso
abbandonato in riva al mare

bisogna eseguire
un movimento ampliando il vuoto
tra il diaframma e gli intercostali
sono ben note le interazioni
con farmaci e con alcolici
o verità esistenziali
(si raccomanda poi l'espirazione)

Madama morte, gentile chanteuse,
Si fa baciare la mano, galante
Dagli intervenuti
(tutti i poeti sono invitati
tutti vestiti alla stessa maniera
la stessa aria noiosa e annoiata
pallidi rigidi e silenziosi)

rit.

Violetta

Violetta,
Stress that haste is precisely
The true danger to weak nerves
then it's enough to go to the pharmacy for
a pain killer or an aspirin
Inspiration® is a slow practice
an exercise in inhalation

refrain   "I would like to have a marble tombstone
            but instead it's styrofoam
            abandoned on the seashore

you need to make
a movement that expands the emptiness
between the diaphragm and the ribs
well known are the interactions
with medicines and with alcohol
or existential truths
(exhaling is then recommended)

Madame death, sweet chanteuse,
She makes all those present
Kiss her hand, so gallant
(all poets are invited
all dressed the same way
the same tedious and bored air
ALL pale stiff and silent)

refrain

CHANDRA LIVIA CANDIANI

Tu tienimi
e io mi trasformerò in meraviglia,
tra le tue mani,
al caldo,
quel caldo che di notte
fa crescere il grano.
Porta
il corpo amato,
come vita segreta –
preservata –
sotto lo spesso ghiaccio
della memoria.
Tu tienimi
come guscio di noce
nel pugno
fessura tra i mondi.
C'è silenzio tra te e me
c'è perla.
Ti tengo.

Hold me
and I will turn into wonder,
in your hands,
in the warmth,
that warmth that by night
makes wheat grow.
Carry
the beloved body,
like a secret life –
preserved –
under the thick ice
of memory.
Hold me
like a walnut shell
in your fist
a crevice among worlds.
There is silence between you and me
there is pearl.
I hold you.

Adesso che non so più niente
che il vuoto è bella dimora
che ho passi senza arsura
che siedo e imparo
a esitare, adesso
che non sei più al centro
e quello che conta non è più
al centro
ma spostato
tra le mani
dove le dita si disarmano
e fanno un gesto limato,
adesso questa categorica bellezza
di rami e cieli
pugnala solo
perché entri luce.

Now that I no longer know anything
that emptiness is a lovely abode
that I have steps without scorching heat
that I sit and learn
to hesitate, now
that you are no longer at the center
and what counts is no longer
at the center
but has moved
between my hands
where my fingers are disarmed
and make a polished gesture
now this categorical beauty
of branches and skies
stabs only
to let the light come in.

Niente, è che a me piacciono da sempre
le cose mute,
quando l'io zittisce
e si alza il volume della voce
non solo degli uccelli
ma anche del silenzio dell'armadio
e del tavolo
della lampada e del letto.
Allora niente,
vivo in una nuvola di luce
dove tutto rabbrividisce
e fa parola, allora bevo
all'orlo del mondo
alla sua fontana.

Well, it's just that I have always liked
mute things,
when the self falls silent
and the volume of voices increases
not just that of birds
but also of the silence of the closet
and the table
the lamp and the bed.
Well then,
I live in a cloud of light
where everything shivers
and makes words, and so I drink
at the edge of the world
at its fountain.

Siamo nuvole
i nomi complicano la tessitura
ma siamo nuvole,
notturne mattiniere
dipende,
oltraggiose spaurite
candide sprezzanti,
cavalieri e cavalcature
bastimenti e animali
siamo pronte
a dissolverci con fierezza
in quel tutto pacatissimo
del cielo ultimo
che ci affida il mondo.
Siamo nuvole
cambiamo vita di frequente
lí, sopra il disordine della realtà
il fondo
sereno delle cose,
la pioggia
la sete.

We are clouds
names complicate the texture
but we are clouds,
nocturnal, early rising
it depends,
insulting fearful
candid scornful,
horsemen and mounts
vessels and animals
we are ready
to fade away boldly
into that all quiet
of the last sky
that entrusts us with the world.
We are clouds
we change lives often
there, above the disorder of reality
the serene
end of things,
rain
thirst.

Allora senti
ci sarà un lupo
e sarà bianco
tu sarai bendata
e gli starai in groppa
in piedi
correrete insieme
slacciàti dalla ragione
legittimi alla velocità dell'aria.
Non ci sarà bisogno di fidarsi
avrà fiuto e tu equilibrio.

Dovrai tener caldo alle parole
tenerle in un orto sotto la camicia
a stretto contatto con la pelle.
Bruceranno e graffieranno.
Lasciati bruciare.

Passerete dalle città
non levarti mai la benda
anche quando sentirai chiamare
lusingare invocare resta dritta
in piedi in groppa al lupo.

La memoria è una fabbrica
che non smette mai
fa i turni di notte e non ha festivi.
Il lupo slaccerà i ricordi
uno per uno ne farà
fiocchi di neve.
Il vuoto sarà vasto
e alto e profondo
lo chiamerai carezza.

Allora senti.

So listen
there will be a wolf
and he will be white
you'll be blindfolded
and you'll be on his back
standing
you will run together
unleashed from reason
lawful at the speed of air.
There will be no need to trust
he will have a knack and you'll have balance.

You'll need to keep the words warm
keep them in a garden under your shirt
in close contact with your skin.
They will burn and scratch.
Let yourself burn.

You will pass by the cities
don't ever remove your blindfold
even when you hear the calling
flattering pleading, stay standing
straight up on the wolf's back.

Memory is a factory
that never stops
it works the night shift and has no holidays.
The wolf will unravel memories
one by one he'll turn them into
snowflakes.
The void will be vast
and tall and deep
you will call it caress.

So listen.

BEPPE SEBASTE

C'è sempre la foto di uno che guarda

Le immagini dell'anno che finisce, / pubblicate sul giornale alla fine di dicembre, / sembrano le stesse pubblicate / l'anno precedente, / oppure dieci, quindici anni prima. / Il senso di saturazione delle immagini del mondo / diventa più forte alla fine / dell'anno, quando i giornali fanno / una specie di festival del selfie, / di ciò che da sempre hanno già pubblicato...

c'è sempre la foto di uno che guarda,
indica un punto all'orizzonte
c'è sempre uno che grida in bianco e nero, la bocca
impaurita, spalancata
c'è sempre quello che si bacia con un'altra, o un altro, che lo bacia
a sua volta, mentre tutti li guardano,
oppure senza che nessuno li guardi
c'è sempre uno in primo piano che solleva una bandiera, uno stendardo, una cosa,
le braccia sopra la testa,
c'è sempre la foto di quello vicino al fuoco che divampa
di quello che brucia (che *arde*)
c'è sempre quello che corre con la figlia o il figlio sulle spalle
e ci sono sempre quelli di schiena che guardano
il mare sporco, il mare bello,
il mare coi soldati sulla spiaggia e le rovine,
c'è sempre il palazzo sventrato, il grattacielo annerito dal fumo,
le crepe nei ghiacciai che si sciolgono
staccandosi dal sonno creduto perenne,
il bosco che arde (che *brucia*) e la gente di spalle che lo guarda,
c'è sempre un Presidente che cammina mano nella mano
con una donna, e sorride, e un attore che si sposa, che sorride,
c'è sempre qualcuno che piange, un bambino in bianco e nero con un
carrarmato sullo sfondo
c'è sempre un adulto con la maglietta sportiva sullo sfondo di detriti
sollevati da un'esplosione, e ci sono
sempre altri adulti con una maglietta sportiva che applaudono,
alcuni con il pugno alzato,
c'è sempre uno con la faccia perplessa, e un altro di cui si vede solo
la nuca, e il vuoto davanti, il vuoto all'orizzonte,

There's always the photo of someone watching

The images of the year that's ending, / published in the newspaper at the end of December, / look the same as those published / the year before, / or ten, fifteen years before. / The sense of saturation of the images of the world / becomes stronger at the end / of the year, when the newspapers hold / a kind of festival of selfies, / of what they've always published already...

there's always the photo of someone watching,
indicating a point on the horizon
there's always someone screaming in black and white, their mouth
afraid, open wide
there's always someone kissing someone else, who is kissing them
back, while everyone is watching,
or without anyone watching
there's always the close up of someone raising a flag, a standard, a thing,
their arms above their head,
there's always the photo of someone near a fire that's flaring up
of someone who's burning (who's *blazing*)
there's always someone who's running with their son or daughter on their shoulders
and there are always those watching with their backs to us
the dirty sea, the beautiful sea,
the sea with soldiers on the beach and the ruins,
there's always the gutted building, the skyscraper blackened by fire,
the cracks in the melting glaciers
breaking off from the sleep thought to be perennial,
the wood blazing (*burning*) and the people with their backs to us watching it,
there's always a President who's walking hand-in-hand
with a woman, and smiling, and an actor who's getting married, who's smiling
there's always someone crying, a child in black and white with a
tank in the background
there's always an adult in a sports shirt in front of the debris
from an explosion, and there are
always other adults with sports shirts who are clapping,
some with their fists raised,
there's always someone with a puzzled face, and another, we just see
his nape, and the void in front, the void on the horizon,

quello che annega nell'acqua azzurra, o sembra che anneghi,
c'è sempre una città che brucia sullo sfondo, il fumo nero
che scorre verso l'alto come un fiume, poi scompare,
le fiamme che divampano, o forse
sono i fuochi d'artificio che colorano la festa,
la festa dell'ultimo anno nuovo, magari il penultimo

(dicembre 2017)

someone drowning in blue water, or seeming to drown,
there's always a city burning in the background, the black smoke
running up like a river, then disappearing,
the flames flaring up, or perhaps
it's the fireworks that color the party,
the party for the last new year, maybe the second to last

(December 2017)

Billy the Kid (La ballata di)

Billy the Kid era una donna si vestiva come un uomo
ma era una donna, era seria e triste,
"seria e triste" perché queste parole le stavano bene addosso
Billy the Kid era abbastanza una bella donna era libera
di camminare e incontrava amici d'infanzia
Billy the Kid non aveva l'infanzia o non si ricordava
di averla
incontrava dovunque amici d'infanzia che si arrendevano
Billy the Kid raramente si arrendeva e quando
lo faceva
dopo si voltava per sparargli
Billy the Kid era libera e camminava era una donna bella
come la stagione dell'infanzia era seria e triste e sorrideva
Billy the Kid cercava dovunque amici d'infanzia e
sorrideva
Billy the Kid era una puttana era bella e triste
non era mai dove credevi che fosse
non era mai dove credeva che fosse
Billy the Kid era una donna si vestiva come un uomo
ma era una donna era seria e triste
Billy the Kid la uccise Pat Garrett un amico d'infanzia
perché Pat Garrett conosceva l'infanzia
e Billy the Kid la conosceva da sempre
che cercava dovunque degli amici d'infanzia e
sorrideva
incontrò Billy the Kid che gli camminava incontro, seria e triste
perché queste parole le stavano bene addosso
Billy the Kid era una donna camminava libera
non era mai dove credeva che fosse
Pat Garrett uccise Billy The Kid un mattino d'infanzia
provarono entrambi una grande tenerezza
provarono entrambi una grande tenerezza

(1993)

Billy the Kid (The ballad of)

Billy the Kid was a woman she dressed like a man
but she was a woman, she was serious and sad, "serious and sad"
because these words fit her well
Billy the Kid was a rather beautiful woman she was free
to walk and meet childhood friends
Billy the Kid had no childhood or she didn't remember
having one
everywhere she met childhood friends who surrendered
Billy the Kid rarely surrendered and after
she did
she would turn around to shoot them
Billy the Kid was free and walked she was a beautiful woman
like the season of childhood she was serious and sad and smiled
Billy the Kid searched for childhood friends everywhere and
smiled
Billy the Kid was a slut she was beautiful and sad
she was never where you thought she was
she was never where she thought she was
Billy the Kid was a woman she dressed like a man
but she was a woman she was serious and sad
Billy the Kid she was killed by Pat Garrett a childhood friend
because Pat Garrett had known childhood
and had known Billy the Kid all along
and searched for childhood friends everywhere and
smiled
he met Billy the Kid who walked up to him, serious and sad
because these words fit her well
Billy the Kid was a woman she walked free
she was never where she thought she was
Pat Garrett killed Billy the Kid one childhood morning
they both felt a great tenderness
they both felt a great tenderness

(1993)

Stanno girando un film

Stanno girando un film.
Non ne sapevamo nulla.
Nel film ci siamo noi e sembriamo
più veri che qui, da dove
lo guardiamo.
Siamo più belli nel film
che fuori dal film.
Poi camminiamo.
Ci viene voglia di andare a casa
ma troviamo delle transenne.
Non si può passare, dice quello in divisa.
Vogliamo tornare a casa, diciamo.
Non si può, siete dentro al film e dal film
non si può uscire. Dovevate pensarci
prima.
Dietro le transenne ci sono camionette
e uomini armati.
E la casa? La casa è in un altro
film, ma è vietato, non
ce lo fanno vedere.
Intanto
stanno girando un altro film.

(2018)

They're Shooting a Movie

They're shooting a movie.
We knew nothing about it.
We're there in the film and we seem
more real than here, from where
we're watching it.
We're more beautiful in the film
than outside the film.
Then we walk.
We feel like going home
but we find some fences.
You can't go through, says someone in a uniform.
We want to go home, we say.
You can't, you're in the film and you can't leave
the film. You should have thought about it
before.
Behind the fences there are vans
and armed men.
And our house? Our house is in another
film, but it's forbidden, they
won't let us watch it.
Meanwhile
they're shooting another film.

(2018)

La O di terra

La O di sogno e di orizzonte
la O di alba che si sveglia
la O rosa e gialla che si alza
e illumina la vasta O di terra
di una luce pastosa come crema al limone O
di zucca – la O di zucca e di limone, la O di luce e
di ombra.
La vocale O è un occhio che guarda ogni cosa
come se la creasse – la O di cosa,
di parola, la O di guardare – una O neonata
che nasce col mondo – la O di mondo,
la grande O di girasole – la O di incanto, la O incantata
di rosa, di cielo, la misteriosa O di iris, di cuore,
la O di scrivere poesie,
la O di anima che ride

The O of Earth

The O of dream and of Open
the O of awakening dawn
the pink and yellow O rising
and lighting up the vast O of earth
in a light mellow as Orange or pumpkin
cream – the O of pumpkin and of Orange, the O of light and
of shade.
The vowel O is an eye watching every thing
as if it created it – the O of things,
of word, of colours, the O of watching, of Off, of Out of time – a newborn O
born with the world – the O of world,
the big O of sunflower – the O of moon, ball, olive tree, the enchanted O
of rose, of sky, the mysterious O of iris, of heart, of song,
the O of writing poems,
the O of laughing soul

Una vita dolce

Piano piano ti avvicini forse alla non esistenza,
alla fine del ciclo, o nei suoi paraggi,
là dove avresti forse la possibilità
di non incarnarti più in una sofferenza di vita
(oh, non adesso, non la prossima morte, lo sai bene)
eppure senti la possibilità che sia stata

              una vita dolce

Alla fine volevi raccontare soltanto una vita
normale,
la tenerezza, l'esistenza è una cosa dolce e non comporta meriti
il non avere dubbi sul camminare, sull'esistere,
nella notte riconoscere gli zampilli di luce
che danno la calma, piccole luci del coraggio
nel buio fitto fitto
punteggiato di diamanti conficcati nella gomma

Piano piano insomma ti avvicini, in modo naturale, alla non esistenza,
alla fine del ciclo o nei suoi paraggi,
alla necessità di incarnarti in una nuova sofferenza di vita
sognando l'estinzione
e il divenire atomo
di cielo

Intanto cammini nel buio e non hai dubbi
sull'esistere,
una vita dolce,
riconosci gli zampilli di luce
che danno la calma
le piccole luci del coraggio nel nero fitto
punteggiato da luci, come diamanti
nella gomma indurita

A sweet life

Gradually you get closer perhaps to nonexistence,
the end of the cycle, or somewhere nearby,
the place where you might have the chance
to no longer be reborn in a life suffering
(oh, not now, not the next death, you know well)
yet you feel the possibility that it's been

                a sweet life

In the end you only wanted to tell of a normal
life,
tenderness, existence is a sweet thing and it brings no rewards
with no doubts about walking, about existing,
in the night recognizing the bursts of light
that bring calm, little lights of courage
in the pitch darkness
dotted with diamonds stuck in gum

Gradually then, you naturally get closer to nonexistence,
to the end of the cycle or somewhere nearby,
to the necessity of being reborn in a new life suffering
dreaming of extinction
and becoming an atom
of the sky

Meanwhile you walk in the dark and you have no doubts
about existing,
a sweet life,
you recognize the bursts of light
that bring calm
the little lights of courage in the pitch dark
dotted by lights, like diamonds
in the hardened gum

NEFELI MISURACA

Viviamo nascosti alla violenza della noia
al corrugarsi del tempo, al computo degli errori,
a quel resto da fare che ci aspetta
alla fine della strada, all'ombra di un ponte improvviso,
in un mare coperto da un muro di pioggia.
Solleviamo la Terra con entrambe le mani,
schivando speranze,
protetti dalla vergogna di essere vivi.

E la morte mi cercherà tra le matte risate,
nel riverbero ostinato di una giornata lontana,
e mi troverà pallida e ferma nel mezzo,
come un capitolo incompiuto.

We live in hiding from the brutalities of boredom
from the furrowing of time, the counting of errors,
from all that is left to do, what's waiting for us
at the end of the road, in the shade of a sudden bridge,
in front of a sea obscured by a wall of rain.
We pull up the Earth with both hands,
dodging all hopes,
protected by the shame of being alive.

And death will look for me while laughing madly
in the unwavering glare of a faraway morning
and she will find me standing pale and still
like an unfinished chapter.

Scoprire il ratto che attraversa le grate,
la sua passeggiata ubriaca per i vicoli dritti,
il suono impastato delle sue zampe sulla strada nera
di questo mondo, di un'altra vita.

Fratello ratto, anche il mio passo
comanda stupore, orrore, ricordo,
come la fame e la sete dei primordi.
Fratello, svicoliamo via senza vergogna.

Quando verrà il giorno,
saluteremo rasente i muri il destino
che ci sorprenderà soli.

A rat grazes through the rusted grates
swerving drunk along straight alleys
his chafing steps on the black concrete
of this world here, of that other existence.

Brother rat, my steps like yours
summon wonder, horror, reminiscence,
ancestral thirst, primordial thrift.
Oh brother, shamelessly we'll stray.

When the day comes,
We'll skirt the walls of a destiny
finding us alone.

Maleducazione dello sguardo, forzi
i confini delle finestre, e affondi
dritta nei mattoni delle case –
e l'immobilità di queste sere arroventate,
quando il verso di un gabbiano discende
da un angolo invisibile del cielo e dice
cose innominabili, piene di urgenza –
e nulla al cospetto degli anni
che tracciano i cerchi nei tronchi.
Il raggio fermo di luce
s'incurva sul pavimento e completa il suo giro
con la calma della terra, consumando
le piastrelle, con un tempo rimane
orfano di queste diciannove e trentuno
del ventisette giugno. Oggi scioperano
gli aeroporti. Si temono meduse sulle coste
del Tirreno. Muoiono decine di persone,
come sempre, da qualche parte del mondo.

O rudeness of my gaze, you burst out
my windows, cutting right
through the bricks of the houses –
and the stillness of these scorching nights,
when a seagull descends gawking
down an invisible corner of the sky, uttering
unspeakable things, full of urgency–
and nothing, compared to the years
that carved circles on tree trunks.
An idle beam of light
lies bending on my floor, closing its cycle
with the slow pace of the earth, wearing out
my tiles, and time
is left orphaned of this seven thirty-one pm
this June twenty-ninth. Today
airports are on strike. Expected waves
of jellyfish on the Tyrrhenian coasts. Dozens of people,
as usual, die somewhere in the world.

La mia macchina mi somiglia
con la sua carrozzeria antiquata, un poco ammaccata
sui fianchi e l'odometro imponderabile.
La mia macchina sorride quando
corre libera nei saliscendi delle colline
e distende la pupilla e il contagiri nelle rincorse a perdifiato.
Invisibile e intemerata quando è sola,
pronta al salto e all'inchino senza preavviso.
La mia macchina mi ricorda
e non chiede nulla che non sia combustibile,
un'infarinatura di oli lubrificanti, e lo spazio
che prefigura la salita, dimentica dello sforzo
e dei nemici nello specchietto retrovisore
perché tutti spariranno, senza un sospiro,
alla prossima felice radura.
La mia macchina mi sorprende
e ripete per sempre la nenia mozartiana
anche di fronte alla betoniera ottusa,
anche dietro al rimorchio senza fari,
anche sospesa sullo scivolo dei ghiacciai
di un inverno senza promesse.

My car looks like me,
with her old-fashioned bodywork, a little dented
around the edges, and her unfathomable odometer.
My car smiles at me,
running carefree up and down the hills,
her eyes and tachometer on a wild ride–
invisible and daring in her lonely runs,
unnoticed while she hiccups and jumps.
My car understands me,
and asks for nothing but gas,
engine oil and the open space
before the climb, ignoring exhaustion
and our enemies, back
in the rear-view mirror
because they all will disappear,
in a blink, by the next clearing.
My car surprises me,
repeating the Mozartian mantra
while tailing a dull rig,
doubling a blind trailer,
swerving on the eternal ice caps
of a winter without promises.

Questa è la vita che ci appartiene,
lo storpio che compare improvviso dietro la curva,
una cisterna vuota su un'impalcatura scrostata,
la luce bianca d'inverno senza il cerchio del sole.
Più nera del sangue, l'ombra del muso di un gatto
buttato per terra con cura gentile, come nel sonno,
con l'occhio annebbiato su quel poco di bianco fra la striscia e la strada
che scolora dai rulli di verniciatura automatica.
Attraversiamo il cumulo di ossa e sussurri
mentre teniamo lo sguardo immobile
su mosche e ondate di sabbia, buste azzurrine, coperchi vuoti.
Essere civilizzati a forza, questa la vita che ci appartiene,
tenendo in equilibrio un libro sulla testa.

This is the life we belong to:
a cripple creeping up unexpected behind a curve,
an empty tank on rusty scaffolding,
the wintry white light without the circle of the sun.
Blacker than blood is the shadow of a cat's muzzle
thrown against the cement with gentle care, as if in her sleep,
its milky eyes staring at the gap between the line and the road
left by the roaring passage of a steamroller.
We cross the hill of bones and whispers
forever gazing intently
at flies and sand dunes, plastic bags, empty lids.
Being forcibly civilized is the life we belong to,
a book wobbling on top of our heads.

CARLO BOASSA

La voce

*Quanto cielo sulle spalle di un uomo,
e stelle che si scaldano le mani
al suo stupore; e come
sotto la fredda luna del suo sguardo
il mare della morte si racqueta;
e come il sangue sparso delle cose
stilla dal fil di lama dei suoi sogni.
Penzola all'albero della bellezza
l'impiccato dicibile,
ma è suo quel collo.*

The Voice

*How much sky on a man's shoulders,
and stars that warm their hands
over his astonishment; and how
under the cold moon of his gaze
the sea of death becalms itself;
and how the spilled blood of things
drips from the cutting edge of his dreams.
From the tree of beauty the
hanged effable swings
but the neck is his.*

Pietà

Ne lo gran mar de l'essere in tempesta
un giorno naufragasti.
Anni si addormentarono, finché
quel giorno si svegliò tra le mie braccia
caldo di bello, vero, come un cristo scolpito
tra quelle di sua madre – o della mia.

Pietà

In the great stormy sea of being
one day you foundered.
Years fell asleep, until
that day woke up in my arms
warm with beauty, true, like a sculpted christ
in the arms of his mother – or of mine.

A Recanagliari

Azzurre di illusione
le cime dei ricordi più lontani.
Panorama: etimologicamente
sono escluso da tutto.

Sempre cara da me l'autoesclusione
mi fu dell'orizzonte;
ma al davanzale oasi
oh mitdasein-Sahara di poetare!

Di salvarmi la morte sul cammello
entro l'ariosa cruna di poetare
passa la mia finestra buoni scalmi
sulle onde del cielo, su quel mare.

At Recanagliari

Blue with illusion
the peaks of the most distant memories.
Panorama: etymologically
I'm excluded from everything.

Always dear to me was the self-exclusion
of the horizon;
but at the windowsill - oasis
oh mitdasein-Sahara of making poetry!

Of saving my death on the camel
in the airy needle eye of making poetry
my window passes good oarlocks
on the waves of the sky, on that sea.

La cagna

Al focolare delle tue viscere
felicità s'accuccia, s'addormenta.
E tu la credi ignara di tutto,
che sia già in paradiso.
Ma basta un tuo sospiro
e lei drizza l'orecchio;
e se tu esci nella notte nera
abbandonando tutto
essa ti seguirà, fedele,
pronta a balzare avanti con un ringhio.

The Dog

*At the hearth of your entrails
happiness lies down, falls asleep
and you believe her unaware of everything
already in paradise.
But one sigh of yours is enough
and she raises her ear;
and if you go out in the dark night
leaving everything
she will follow you, faithfully,
ready to spring forward with a growl.*

Principia pathematica II

Stando attento a non calpestare monumenti
sui due passi slacciati non inciampi
come chi ruba le vecchie bende di Lazzaro
l'ubriaco d'angoscia.
Rendano gli occhi solide
copiose lacrime di indifferenza.

Principia Pathematica II

Carefully avoiding stepping on monuments
let the man drunk with anxiety
not trip over the two unlaced steps
like those who steal Lazarus's old bandages.
Let the eyes render solid
abundant tears of indifference.

FABIO ORECCHINI

al dire lontano

che fu sapersi detta, circoscritta nella forma o figura appena pronunciata,
figurante asservita alla scena appena trascorsa -evocata- *qualcuno provi a
soccorrermi a sfigurarmi*

almeno, figurarsi altrove

dopo nei giorni

ritrovi ancora schegge -parti di parti di un discorso- o più semplicemente *ora, la
gola è un gelo* l'arcata del cielo non detiene, le viscere calde amputate sul
pavimento e poi il lutto

pulire ciò che detto, le parole buttate sul letto

non sia più che un'ombra

to say from afar

that it was known to be called, circumscribed in the form or figure barely pronounced, appearing enslaved to the scene just passed-evoked- *someone try to help me to disfigure myself*

at least, imagine yourself elsewhere

after in the days

you still find splinters- pieces of pieces of a conversation- or more simply *now*, *the throat is a chill* the arch of the sky doesn't hold, the hot dismembered innards on the floor and then the grief

to clean up what was said, the words tossed on the bed

it can't be more than a shadow

a volto scoperto, l'interfaccia non richiesto, sogno della mano dei ciechi o rosaspina, dalle foglie d'ombra
il luogo nel *luogo detto del cranio* funesto sia il dire - il vedere scherno- la parola un silenzio intravisto non
una destinazione al respiro, *per i restanti vivi*

l'aria, è sempre un dopo

Il corpo muove a lato

disabilitato, la testa cade sulla destra precipita dal collo -non resta- che un'ombra
percepita -anch'essa si frantuma- *mi chiedi d'essere di tornare*

in vita, spunta dal collo un'altra testa senza vita

corpi e teste semoventi

tracciate con la linea della mano *o che si cercano*

essenti, nel culmine delle braccia

adunate, a margine del dire

portano alla bocca dicerie, se non quando *domani cadrà* dietro l'occhio dentro lo specchio *mal vista* la
mano scompare, un vuoto oltre il braccio

a disdire, la forbice se esce dal polso

barefaced, unrequested communication, dream the hand of the blind or
little briar rose, from the shadow the place *in the place called the cranium* foreboding to say- to see
mockery- the word a silence glimpsed not a destination towards breath, *for the remaining living*

the air, always comes later

The body moves to the side

deactivated, the head falls to the right collapsing from the neck- does not rest- that a shadow
sensed- even that shatters – *you ask me to be* to return

alive, another head pushed from the neck without life

self-propelled bodies and heads

traced with the line of the hand *or they look for each other*

beings, on the summit of the arms

gatherings, at the edges of speech

they bring rumors to the mouth, if not when *tomorrow it will fall* behind the eye
inside the mirror *poorly viewed* the hand disappears, an emptiness beyond the arm

to deny, the scissors if they come out of the wrist

a futura sutura, l'anima eretta che incista, polvere nida in fessura, fissa nel taglio delle mura, oltrepasso,
mite morsura, *ora canta ora scura*, fonte, argine,

screpolatura

d'aria ifigènia, quella notte, molta notte aspettare, uncinare, tenere i fili a nodi, *ora bianca ora scura*,
possibile salita al sole,   anodi,   fenditura

al cappio
al cappio
al cappio

asole infila, cucite le dita in preghiera, vermine, legaccio   annoda   a futura sutura

to the future suture, the erect soul that encysts, dust nested in a fissure, fixed in the crack of the wall, overstep, meek cutting, *now sing now dark*, spring, embankment,

cracking

from the air, iphigenia, that night, to wait many nights, to hook, to hold the strings in knots, *now white now dark*,
possible rise to the sun,   anodes, crevice

in a noose
in a noose
in a noose

eyelets passed through, sew the hands in prayer, vermin, string   knot for a future suture

a svellere trame di rami con crani
frane ténere come cancrene d'uomo
muti incauti s'addentrano i cani
scavando in dentro, il cedimento:
mani   su   mani

rimami rimani
questo infinito tenère

to tear away plots of branches with skulls
tender landslides as gangrene of man
the careless mute dogs advance
digging in the subsidence:
hands   on   hands

rhyme me remain
this infinite hold

madre a nascondere i polsi, le artriti
dei legamenti, il nodo ritorto dei legami
l'incedere a passi lenti sommovimenti,
padre a mostrare i denti, i lacerti, incerto
se ridiscendere verso i catrami mostrami
il martirio di pose le forze arrese, i reperti
non per trascinarsi -iridescente-non per non dire
i come ancora i se resti - *resisti* -
ridere di quanto vissuto per niente

mother to hide the wrists, arthritis
of ligaments, the twisted knot of bonds
walking with slow moving steps,
father to show teeth, the rumps, uncertain
if you go down to the tars show me
martyrdom of poses the surrendered forces, the finds
not to drag on - iridescent - not to say nothing
of things as still as if you remain - *resist* -
laugh at what you experienced for nothing

FRANCA MANCINELLI

In attesa di perdere quota

Nel ripetersi di giorni a formare una sequenza: l'attesa, lo scadere della data. La partenza.

*

A casa i documenti – comandano. Poche frazioni di secondo. E riprendo il governo dei miei gesti. (Conosco gli emissari della paura). Tutto è con me. Richiudo la borsa, trascino la valigia.
Mi risveglierò su un'altra terra. Accanto a questo corredo custodito.

*

Giubbotto galleggiante, maschera di ossigeno, uscite luminose. Una salvezza mimata, con quanta esattezza ripetuta. Le braccia a indicare direzioni opposte, possibili nello stesso istante.

*

Waiting to Lose Altitude

In the repetition of days to form a sequence: the waiting, a date's expiration. The departure.

*

At home the documents - they command. A few fractions of a second. And, I preside over my gestures again. (I know the emissaries of fear). Everything is with me. I close my bag, I drag my suitcase.
I will wake up in another land. Next to this guarded trousseau.

*

Life jacket, oxygen mask, luminous exits. A mimed salvation, with so much repeated exactitude. Arms pointing in opposite directions, possible at the same moment.

*

*

Di una mappa: isole premute con un dito e le parole *ho visto*, *sono andato*, e altri verbi che conducono il moto, che contengono lo stare. Punti circoscritti d'esperienza – l'oceano dell'immaginato sciaborda, avanza e rientra in risacca.

*

Questa foto prova la tua presenza qui. In una luce primaverile il tuo contorno è apparso contro queste mura squadrate, sbrecciate dal tempo. Sorridevi – eri riuscito a sfuggire di un passo. Poi subito rientrato nella scia.

*

*

About a map: islands pressed with a finger and the words *I saw*, *I went*, and other verbs that conduct motion, that contain being there. Circumscribed points of experience – the ocean of the imagined laps, advances and returns in the undertow.

*

This photo proves your presence here. In a spring light your outline appeared against these square walls, chipped by time. You smiled – you managed to escape just barely. Then quickly faded into the wake.

*

In attesa di prendere quota o di perderla. Il proprio nome leggibile ben oltre il biglietto. Gli oggetti più cari trascelti, custoditi.

*

Stringi in pugno qualcosa, a un tratto lo lasci cadere. Si compone un paesaggio di campi, città come ceneri di un fuoco antico. Fiumi in cammino, in fuga come animali sorpresi da un tremito.

*

Montagne, rughe della gioia – pensieri sulla fronte della terra.
Nostro geometrico disporci entro dettati e trame. Nostro irradiarci.

Il pasto va mangiato. O ti risucchia il vuoto.

***

Waiting to gain altitude or to lose it. One's name readable far beyond the ticket. The dearest objects chosen, safeguarded.

*

Your fist clenches something, suddenly you drop it. A landscape of fields appears, cities like ashes from an ancient fire. Rivers on their way, fleeing like animals surprised by a tremor.

*

Mountains, wrinkles of joy – thoughts on the forehead of the earth.
Our geometric disposition within dictates and plots. Our radiating selves.

The meal must be eaten. Or the void sucks you in.

***

Padre, madre, figlio. Le mani sulle spalle, i fianchi uniti. Dietro di loro un luogo che sarà ricordato. Tu che transiti scompari più veloce che puoi. Devi restare fuori dal quadro.

Oppure guardali – stretti nell'obiettivo, dentro l'angolazione giusta. E per favore, scatta.

Father, mother, child. Hands on shoulders, joined hips. Behind them a place that will be remembered. You who transit disappear as fast as you can. You must stay out of the picture.

Or look at them – still in the lens, inside the correct angle. And please, take the picture.

FABIO DONALISIO

nella norma

fine normale   diceva   normalmente
finita; la norma è vita: sparizione,
pure:

        trasferire l'esperienza della norma   diceva,
        nelle consolanti stanze della forma

estrazione della vita dalle cose dure,
o piuttosto dalle forme degli esseri
associati   avariati piuttosto, economicamente
        incontrollati;

            funziona come   diceva
    una memoria,

auctoritas, non veritas, facit legem

auctoritas, non veritas, facit legem

within the norm

a normal end   it was said   normally
ended; the norm is life: disappearance,
too:

           usher the experience of the norm
           into the soothing rooms of form   it was said,

extraction of life from the hard things,
or rather from the forms of associated
beings   *rotten actually, economically*
           unchecked;

               works as
         a memory,   it was said

(prima che si sapesse cosa sia, cosa
possa essere)

                                    una fossa comune
                                    dove interrare il rimosso
                                    che poi filtra, si dà alla terra
                                    e rispunta, fuori come un fiore separato
                                    fragile colosso

il codice è voce   diceva   *prima*
del segno, già deperimento, nuce
dell'arbitrario insegnamento; luogo
di stoccaggio dello sdegno, che muta *poi*
in divieto, interdetto, punizione   *che la forza è nulla*   diceva
                                          senza coagulo,
                                          concrezione

con il moderno sorge il camuffo   *necessario*
la prestidigitazione; alla voce
sopraggiungono le mani, la ressa
dell'azione; la legge il copione   *la casa tribunale,*
della scena   *la cosa pena*   d'altronde,   diceva
                                          (crea)

che vita possibile senza l'arena, senza
lo spazio della pena, che legittima
il movimento, il rito della vittima
e del suo scontento?   *suo nel senso di proprio?*

*

(before it was known what it is, what it could be)

    a mass grave
    where the repressed can be buried
    to then seep down, give itself to the earth
    and re-emerge, rising like a flower apart
    fragile colossus

the code is a voice   it was said   before
the sign, instant atrophy, cradle
of arbitrary teachings; site   then
for storing disdain, that mutates   that force is nothing   it was said
into ban, prohibition, punishment,   without clotting
    accretion

with modernity springs disguise,   necessary
the magic act; to the voice
come the hands, the crush
of the action; the law the script   the house turns court
of the scene   the sentence thing   besides,   it was said

what life without the chamber, without   (creates)
the sentence space, that legitimizes
movement, the rite of victims   their, *meaning* their own?
and their discontent?

*

(coro)

la cosa che diventa bene,
vale solo in quanto si tiene
la cosa che diventa bene
vale solo in quanto si tiene

[non c'è bisogno, in ultima analisi, di una motivazione per lasciare la partita; tre sul tavolo da quattro, tanto per dire, e l'ultimo invitato tenta ancora di capire]

*

(chorus)

things becoming goods
only valued in an owning mood
things becoming goods
only valued in an owning mood

[there is no need, in the last analysis,
for a reason to quit
the game; three at a table for four,
so to speak, and the last guest
still tries to understand]

*

il nodo della proprietà:

                                         diceva

fate il vostro gioco
ne avete – formalmente – diritto
qualcuno in qualche tempo
l'ha messo per iscritto; dunque
possedete, ad libitum, iterum,
al tempo infinito, reclamate
l'oggetto – interamente – smarrito;
e se vale quel che tiene, da chi
il primo bene?

sta facendo tardi   diceva
in questo spazio dove intorno
c'è qualcosa dappertutto; colmare
il divario prima che si faccia lutto,
l'umido asciutto

                                         (già sospetto)

il trattato è stato firmato, con segni
del tutto astratti: se ne traggono parafrasi
ed estratti, margini e commenti, ligi
ad applicare alle cose fatte eventi

ma la norma – a detta dei più alti
competenti – è rimasta fuori, si
teme, del tutto esterna agli esperienti:

"anche in assenza, improvvisamente,
tutto appare muoversi in modo
intelligente; *at modo alibi* qualcosa

the quandary of owning:

play your game
you have – lawfully – the right
someone at some time
wrote it down; so
you possess, ad libitum, iterum,
in the infinite, reclaim
the object – wholly – lost;
and if only what is owned is valued, from whom
the first good?

it's getting late it was said
in this space where all around
there's something throughout; bridge
the gap before it turns to mourn,
moisture to stone

the treaty was signed, with signs
so abstract; spawning paraphrases,
excerpts, margins and comments, faithfully
applied to things turned events

but the norm – according to the highest
authorities – was left out, it is
feared, entirely external to the experient:

"yet even in absence, suddenly,
everything seems to move
knowingly; *at modo alibi* something

it was said

(already doubtful)

FABIO DONALISIO   141

smette, approccia l'inesistente; ed è
li che il contratto   diceva   diventa
nullo e poi niente, mera teoria: ovvero
concepire che qualcosa vada via"

auctoritates, sempre, dunque: sovrano
è colui che decide in modo definitivo
se questo stato di normalità regna
davvero, oppure: non esiste più realismo
perché non esistono più re

la fai facile: *situare se stessi nel diritto,*
a spese di altre porzioni di umanità; questo
diceva; *ottenere ricompensa politica*
al possesso legale della forza; regnare,
diceva colui che pensa, a forza di pensiero
in assoluta castità: diceva *proprio*

ends, approaches the non-existent; and it is
there that the contract   it was said   becomes
null and then nothing, mere theory: that is,
conceive that something can cease to be"

auctoritates, always, then: sovereign
is he who decides definitively
if this state of normality reigns
for real, or: there is no more realism
since there are no more kings

you make it easy: *situate yourself in the right,*
at the expense of other portions of humanity; so
it was said; *gain political reward*
to lawful possession of power; to rule,
said he-who-thinks, through sheer thought
in absolute chastity: it was said

per davvero

con le proprie forze, diceva, per dire
parole con forza di legge, scritte solo
perché si possano leggere, perché
esista la norma, si possano ripetere
in quanto forma; tutto ritorna

re senza realismo, allora,
destino dei reali senza pari

... questo lo diceva l'uomo del balcone
evocatore di binari...

che se lo stato fa eccezione avrà
pur da esserci una norma, sovranamente
installata, da scardinare, solo per potersi
dare il fatto della decisione;

va da sé   diceva   è questo fatto
a far del re il signore; senza, non c'è
potere né maggiore né minore

il gran riportatore del normale, colui
che traghetta dall'eccesso al limite,
al confine; colui che situa nel diritto
grazie e in pegno di potere; gli è dato
dai normodotati pur ignari di tale
dote:

vuolsi così colà dove si puote   diceva

*

for real

with one's forces, it was said, to say
words with the force of law, written only
so they can be read, so
there be a norm, they can be repeated
as form; everything comes back round

rex without realism, then,
fate of peerless royals

... said the man from the balcony
summoner of tracks...

so if the state is an exception
there must surely be a norm, sovereignly
installed, to dismantle, if only to allow
the act of deciding;

no need to say   it was said   this fact
makes the king the ruler; else there be no
power, greater or lesser

the great restorer of the normal, he who
ferries from excess to the edge,
to the brink; he who voices the law
wielder and tool of power,
loaned to him by the
able-bodied unaware of their gift:

vuolsi così colà dove si puote   *it was said*

*

(coro)

*che il mondo, con l'evoluzione
delle polizie, dei documenti,
della radiotelefonia, delle dogane
rende irreparabile qualsiasi
errore della giustizia – oh, mestizia
che il mondo etc*

*adeste, perseguitati
mai più sarete lasciati,
soli*

*

(chorus)

that the world, with the evolution
of police, of documents,
of radiotelephony, of customs
renders irreparable every
error of justice – oh, sorrow
that the world etc

adeste, persecuted
nevermore will you be left,
alone

*

l'essenza dello stato è la paura   diceva
se stesso: un pensiero normalmente distruttivo,
quindi vero; verificarlo il compito del non
paziente, del *contra quem*, dello straniero

di

diceva   *il carattere è – regolarmente –*
fittizio, nel senso di: fingere è finzione
così come persona è maschera; parola
cala nella legge come lupo muto per
la fame in mezzo al gregge: la comunità
– concordemente – prospera, si svolge

il valore degli interessi, semplicemente,
a un certo punto (quando, non è tempo
saputo) venne fissato, divenne giudizio e
giurisdizione; fu costruzione prima che
costruire, si disse diritto prescindendo
il proprio stesso divenire (e qui il tempo
si fece – immediatamente – remoto

diceva)   *la norma semplicemente vige,*
                 periplo e fondamenta di se stessa,
                 permette prima di essere

permessa

aliquem piget   diceva, sornione

poi, è solo perfezionamento tecnico,
prevedibilità e culto della repressione;
dopo le esaltanti parole – poietiche –
di ogni fondazione, una vita
di esiliati dalla passione   chiosava,

the essence of the state is fear   it was said
itself: a normally destructive thought,
thus true; to check the task of the non
patient, the *contra quem*, the stranger

of

it was said   character is – officially –
fictitious, in the sense of: feigning is fiction
just as persona is mask; word
sinks in the law like a wolf silenced by
hunger amidst the herd: the community
– unanimously – prospers, unfolds

the value of interests, simply,
at a certain point (when, time
unknown) was cast, became judgement and
jurisdiction; constructed before
its construction, declared itself right despite
its own mutating (and here time
turned – immediately – remote

it was said)

the norm simply holds,
enclosure and foundation of itself,
allowing before being
allowed

aliquem piget   it was said, slyly

then, it is mere technical mastery,
predictability and cult of repression;
after the rousing words – poietic –
of every foundation, a geological life
exiled from passion   *glossed,*

l'occhio umido del giurista in vista
di pensione,

un freno, almeno, una mano
non la si venga a raccontare

mai dolce
vero soccorso

la sua: sia i fiori sia
le opere di bene

*

(coro)

c'è troppo futuro di niente nella morte,
ne basterebbe molto meno
cataste di morti mica avran pensato
e detto solo invano; fatto, sta
che quando si dovrà proprio
andare, naufragare nel vero
mare, verrà la legge
a dire cosa si deve a chi resta,
come tumulare, dove compitare,
prima che il prete, impietosamente,
chiami la persona buona, la maschera
sciolta addosso a chi la tiene:

the moist eye of the jurist soon
to retire

*

(chorus)

there's too much future of nothing in death, a brake, at least, a hand
much less would be quite enough
throngs of the dead would hardly have thought
or just said in vain; the fact is don't go telling
that when one must truly
move on, founder in the deepest never sweet
sea, the law shall come real rescue
to say what is owed to those who remain,
how to bury, where to spell out,
before the priest, mercilessly, his own: both wreaths and
calls the person good, the mask good deeds
melting upon the wearer:

[fuori tuona, strano per la stagione]

*

[fuori onda]

le cose sono le cose, e l'uomo non è l'uomo

che dunque prima dell'uomo avvenga un nesso relativo? non sappiamo, non lo nego, dopotutto di animale, sociale, trattasi; *contra*: a che pro tutto il *nostro* disquisir di legge?

presumiamo la morte (per assenza), il cadavere manca, ignoriamo il momento del decesso; sappiamo che visse, latita il movente; riguardo all'esperienza del passaggio, siamo in alto mare...

omettesti un "che" prima dell'uomo, precisione, citando, prego

sulla formazione della realtà, vorrai dire, se il dire regge a tanta vanità, a impianto indiziario sì lasco e lacunoso, o meglio: disperante

non sarà per noia che tentiamo di ordinare, sapere il tempo per farlo passare

[thunder outside, strange for this season]

*

[speakers off]

things are things, and man is not
man

you omitted the "only" before
man, precision, when citing,
please

so then before man comes
a relative bond? we don't know,
I can't deny, after all it's an animal,
a social one; *contra*: to what end
all *our* arguing over the law?

on the formation of reality,
you mean to say, if saying can bear
such vanity, a circumstantial system
so lax and lacking, or rather:
dismaying

let us presume death (*in absentia*),
the corpse is missing, we know not the moment
of death; we know he lived, the motive
escapes us; as for the experience
of passing, we are totally lost....

it won't be out of boredom if we try
to tidy up, to know the time
to make it pass

la norma   la forma

la legge   il gregge

poi rispetto a noi

fatalità della rima, di chi   sempre che prima significhi
ci arriva prima   prima e, rispetto a cosa, poi....

the norm

the form

the word

the herd

fate of the rhyme, of who
takes his time given that time means
time and, with respect to what, then

['cause]

then respect to us

GINEVRA LILLI

Noi tutti, rabdomanti
portiamo
senza saperlo
più mondi sottopelle,
più compassioni.

(Fiumicino, 30 dicembre 2016)

We all, diviners
carry
more worlds under our skin,
more compassion,
all without knowing.

(Fiumicino, December 30, 2016)

Per Francesco Moschini

Persa in quell'angolo
che serra
il giorno nella notte,
che spegne con lentezza
la luce,
in quel momento
affilato, io ti voglio
vicino.
Sigaretta tra le mani
rinchiuse
come due chiese,
suore sorelle
lì a pregare. Le nostre abitudini
si tengono compagnia
anch'esse e si sfiorano
in una cerimonia simile a gesti
compiuti
in un tempio.

Fiumicino, 30 dicembre 2016

For Francesco Moschini

Lost in a corner
that bolts
day into night,
that dims
light slowly,
in that sharp moment
I want you
near me.
Cigarette in your hands,
closed-in
like two churches,
sister-nuns
praying. Our habits too
keep each other company
barely brushing
in a ceremony like gestures
performed
in a temple.

Fiumicino, December 30, 2016

In questi giorni
senza misericordia
mi sento macerare
come carta nell'acqua
buttata a camminare
tra i vicoli
mentre tutto,
dentro, lento,
si aggiusta.

Roma, 23 luglio 2015

In these days
without mercy
I feel myself steeping
like paper in water
thrown to walk
the alleys
while everything,
within, slowly
sorts itself out.

Rome July 23, 2015

per Elena Giulia Rossi

Nemmeno
più la forma
sarà più forma.
Questo che vedi
non lo puoi toccare.
Non puoi baciare
queste labbra
pixel.
Si accendono.
Si spengono
con l'interruttore.
Amore vulnerabile.
Amore impossibile.
Impossibile
sentire la superficie.
Non si sedimenta
il tempo. Né la polvere.
Dove saranno
i musei di un domani
se non nel nostro stupore?

(Marano, Tolfa, 30 maggio 2015)

For Elena Giulia Rossi

Not even
form
will be form anymore.
What you see
you cannot touch.
You cannot kiss
These pixel
lips.
They turn on.
They turn off
with a switch.
Vulnerable love.
Impossible love.
It's impossible
to feel the surface.
Time doesn't sediment.
Neither does dust.
Where will the museums
of tomorrow be
if not in our wonder?

(Marano, Tolfa, May 30, 2015)

I migranti

Le vostre urla attutite
non ci giungono
che qualche secondo
al giorno.
Le nostre tovaglie
sono bianche,
Il vostro sangue
non macchia.
E quando proseguirete
(fiume in fuga
impazzito)
noi tutti
non avremo
che imparato
a scandire meglio
il nome delle nostre
paure. In attesa
del vostro perdono.

(Murta Maria, 4 settembre 2015)

Migrants

Your muffled screaming
only reaches us
for a few seconds
a day.
Our tablecloths
are white.
Your blood
doesn't stain.
And when you continue
(fleeing river
crazed)
we all
will only
have learned
to better spell out
the name of our
fears. Waiting for
your forgiveness.

(Murta Maria, September 4, 2015)

GIANNI D'ELIA

La vita in rima

Tutto è il rimare della vita e nulla
Vuole che sia se non il vero e il canto
Che nel ritmare insonne sempre culla
All'onda del verso il male e l'incanto

Life in Rhyme

The rhyme of this life is all things and nothing
Else ever should be: only truth, only song,
Ceaselessly rocking in rhythm unsleeping
On soft waves of verses seduction and wrong

Il rientro

Niente più di questo ritorno lento
Per le strade risapute e in salita
Prima della Porta che imbuca il centro
Al pedale dà il senso della vita

Adesso un altro è davanti e gli tiene
Dietro il padre che pur comanda sempre
Se in avanscoperta tra le ombre estreme
Entrò a mostrarci il silenzioso assente

La bitta ornata dal trifoglio nuovo
Profuma al tardo sole di banchina
El Chiusòt con la pipa è ancora al molo
Seduto a poppa alla MAFALDA in cima

Le casette smaltate di polvere d'oro
Mentre l'ALTROVE riattracca lanciando la cima
Nell'acqua smerigliata senza l'ombra loro
Versicolori alla luce divina

Tremano nel gran serale ristoro
Per chi rientra dal porto in cucina
E trova il pane fatto col lavoro
Come si fanno le parole in rima

Quel rosa del tramonto tra le dita
Su una ronzante bici nera e pigra

Going Home

Nothing more than a slow ride home—
Up well-known streets that climb the hill
Before the gates to the center of town—
Brings the pedals to life. Still,

A different man, now, is riding up front,
His father's behind, with an arm round his waist;
He's still in charge, though, if only as scout
For our silent return to the deepening shades.

There's a bollard adorned with fragrant new clover
Scenting the evening sun on the pier;
El Chiusòt with his pipe sits in the *Mafalda*,
Still there by the docks with the dusk drawing near.

Beside cottages burnished with powdered gold
The *Elsewhere* ties up at the end of its run;
Along the glazed water their colors glow bright
In the last divine light of the soft slanting sun.

They quiver there for the ones going home
For the evening meal, in kitchens with bread
Made with work that is much the same
As the work of the hands that make poems instead.

The sunset clutched in hand like a rose
The whir of a bicycle, black and slow.

Sul portone

La casa che abitiamo da trent'anni
Ha l'ingresso davanti ad una chiesa
E riuscendo e rientrando a gioie e affanni
Risenti gente che lì canta e prega

Grida e brusii di nozze e funerali
Lagne e fruscii di scarpe e processioni
Queruli crocchi di Pasque e Natali
Messe domenicali e devozioni

Santa Lucia che al tredici dicembre
Così piccola è tutta un gran viavài
Per tanti cuori di città affluente
A benedir gli occhi e salvar dai guai

Quando rientra dai suoi cari giri
Nei luoghi aperti dove sente il sacro
Tra rimorso e rimpianto pare miri
Quel portone che mai più ha varcato

Preso dai bei desiri e dai sospiri
Anche il poeta al buon Cristo educato
Mentre risvetta nuda agli ebbri stridi
La croce contro il cielo tramontato

Se sola fede è il lungo non sapere
Ai brevi anni che restano e alle sere

By the Entranceway

Through the house where we've lived for thirty years
Drift the sounds of a church's entranceway,
Of people bringing their joys and fears,
Coming and going to sing and pray.

The cries of weddings and funerals,
Wails and the shuffle of shoes in processions,
Querulous crowds at festivals,
Sunday masses and Easter devotions.

In the little church on St. Lucy's day,
Beneath December's darkening skies,
A river of souls flows through to pray
For the patron saint's blessing upon their eyes.

The sacred's outdoors in the open air,
He feels: yet still regret and loss,
When on his loved walks he passes there
That threshold which he does not cross.

They raise the cross, bare, against dusk-red skies
And the poet too, with his Christian education,
Hearing the faithful's ecstatic cries,
Is filled with fine yearning by their jubilation.

As if faith alone grants us grace to ignore
Our few years left, the evening at the door.

La cena

Sale ogni sera l'odore della cena
Come un ospite invisibile le scale
Ed ogni vivanda rallegra e rivela
Del tempo andato il senso abissale

Dalla madre alla moglie l'amido dei funghi
Si spande come il bosco sui pendii
Come il ricordo breve d'anni lunghi
Riesce il ragazzo cercatore ai rii

Ecco piselli zucchine melanzane
Risvegliarsi nell'arso dei soffritti
Richiamando le pietanze lontane
Le mille volte in cui mangiammo zitti

Come l'aroma di brace nella via
Tra i suoni assidui con la Musa accanto
Porta la sera la cena e la magia
Cara e dolce fragranza d'ogni incanto

Anche se tutto dice che noi andremo via
E quarant'anni son scoccati in un lampo

Supper

The smell of supper comes up the stairs
Every night an invisible guest;
Each dish is cheering and each dish bears
A sense of the void of time past.

The fragrance of mushrooms, from mother to wife
Stretches down like the slope of a wood;
Once again there's a boy at the dawn of his life,
Foraging down by the brook.

Chopped onion with carrot and celery in oil
Brings eggplant to life as it simmers,
And evokes long-past meals that we still recall,
Our thousands of silent dinners.

The smell of a wood-fired grill in the street,
Its sounds, with my muse waiting near,
Conjures up evenings and past suppers sweet,
A fragrant spell cast in the air.

Even if everything speaks of our end
And how forty years vanish to nothing

La Musa

Lei sì fu subito l'ultima spiaggia
Dopo i balocchi di rivolte e ebbrezze
La pace ritrovata nella saggia
Quotidiana bontà di tenerezze

Come una manna discesa dal cielo
A sfamare e dissetare il disperso
A togliere dal cuore il gran veleno
Con l'amore del lavoro e del verso

Parlò la Musa e fu una luna piena
Bianco sorriso nella notte nera
Grazia d'ascolto e consiglio che calma
Costanza del tempo e compagna speranza

Cara Annalisa della nuova vita
Dopo il gran torto di un amore morto
Per sempre accanto al fare e mai divisa
Al naufrago conforto e vero porto

Lei sola dentro al cosmo e nella stanza
Dolce viso di Madonna che incanta
Lei sola tra l'urlante tracotanza
Calda voce che sussurra e che canta

Il suono onesto tra cosa e emozione
Per l'aria viva e sorella del nome

The Muse

And all at once, she was my final harbor,
Beyond delirious games and insurrections;
My peace new-found within a quiet ardor,
A wise and daily goodness of affection.

Like manna sent to earth, sweet heaven's art
To feed the wanderer and quench his thirst,
To cleanse the poison from his weary heart,
With love of labor and with love of verse.

The Muse spoke, and behold, the moon waxed full,
A candid smile in night's deep black enskied;
A listening grace, and counsel that does still
My mind; steadfast through time, hope by my side.

Beloved Annalisa, my new life,
Past trials and wrongs of a love cut short;
My succor in work, my stay against strife,
The castaway's comfort, and his true port.

In verse and universe, she stands alone,
A sweet-faced Madonna who all enchantment brings;
She stands alone 'midst this world's noisy pride,
A voice that whispers warm, a voice that sings,

'Twixt thing and feeling, honesty's clear vein
Through living air, the sister of her name.

CESARE VIVIANI

XX.

C'è un modo delle persone attente, prudenti,
di lasciarsi andare all'improvviso al pericolo,
di subire una truffa, di affondare
nella più disarmata e innocente ingenuità.
Si sa: anche nella migliore quotidianità,
nelle migliori famiglie,
scompare l'intensità dell'amore, la passione feconda,
l'espansione della forza, si assottiglia
l'energia vitale. Allora quando un impostore
telefona o si avvicina o fa vibrare le corde
di una felice intesa, di un'adesione piena,
di un favore assoluto e indiscutibile della sorte,
di una protezione totale, oh era questo che aspettavamo
da sempre nel grigiore delle giornate, non si può
non aprire il cuore e gioire!

XX.

There is a way that attentive, prudent
people have of yielding suddenly to danger,
of being swindled, of sinking into
the most disarming and innocent naïveté.
No doubt: even in the best daily routine,
in the best families,
the intensity of love disappears, the fertile passion,
the expansion of strength, vital energy
grows thin. So when an impostor
phones or comes close or plucks the strings
of a favorable accord, of a full partaking,
of an absolute and indisputable favor of destiny,
of a total protection, oh this is what we had always
been waiting for in the grey of our days, the heart
can only open and rejoice!

(Oh c'è qualcuno che pensa ancora
che ci sia un modo di scrivere di sé non patetico!
Ma tutte le abilità, i travestimenti, le ironie,
gli artifici, gli sforzi compiuti
per allontanare il patetico, lo avvicinano).

Non sopportava Nicola coloro che usano
la preghiera come una tessera,
o gli altri che, dicendosi artisti,
formano una famigliola di reciproci elogi.
Non sopportava che l'ardore fosse tramutato in conforto,
il coraggio in consolazione.

Non sopportava la *web generation*. La vedeva
come la massima espressione dell'avidità,
tutta rivolta a velocità e rendimento:
ora superata anche la visibilità,
come dispersione narcisistica e forma
di voracità ancora impacciata e palese,
ogni energia si riversava in capacità di lavoro,
l'avidità diventava più compatta e scientifica.
E in questa generazione digitale –
Nicola, che usava la penna, era chiaramente
specie in via d'estinzione –
le donne prevalevano – altro motivo
di disapprovazione per lui -, perché convertivano
in capacità di costruzione
tutta la loro ricchezza affettiva.

Oh fosse data adeguata importanza
all'irrigidimento delle fasce muscolari,
alle contratture! E si cogliesse
quale profondo significato,
quale pericolo si nasconde
in questi all'apparenza semplici disagi!

(Oh there is someone who still thinks
there is a non-pathetic way of writing of oneself!
But all abilities, disguises, ironies,
artifices, efforts performed
to keep the pathetic at bay, bring it closer).

Nicola couldn't tolerate those who make use of
prayer as if it were a card,
or others who, like self-proclaimed artists,
form a neat little family of reciprocal praise.
He couldn't tolerate that the fervor was transformed into comfort,
courage into consolation.

He couldn't stand the web generation. He saw it
as the utmost expression of greed,
ever tending toward speed and production:
now that even visibility was surpassed,
like a narcissistic dispersion and form
of voracity still awkward and evident,
every energy was directed toward work capacity,
greed became more compact and scientific.
And in this digital generation –
Nicola, who used a pen, was clearly
a dying breed –
women prevailed – another reason
for disapproval in his view -, because they converted
all of their emotional richness
into building capacity.

Oh if only adequate importance were given
to the stiffening of the muscular bands,
to contractures! And if only one could know
what deep meaning,
what danger is hidden
in these seemingly banal discomforts!

La severità di Nicola rimarcava astiosa
ogni difetto, non perdonava
la debolezza, l'incertezza,
l'approssimazione, la distrazione.
Oh se le avesse viste, invece, come cicatrici indelebili
di colpi subiti,
se le avesse perdonate o, meglio ancora, amate
come ferite di guerra, come segni inevitabili
di inevitabili traversate!

Questi studiosi che di ogni convegno fanno
un'esibizione di preparazione e di capacità!
E mostrano di sapere e fanno del sapere
una discriminazione tra intelligenti e no,
questi studiosi, quando dovranno
varcare l'ultima porta, come si scopriranno
impreparati!
Nicola non sopportava il beato sorriso
di chi si sente, grazie all'intelligenza, avanti.

Esaurita la riserva di compassione,
non c'è guerra, non c'è disgrazia,
non c'è agghiacciante notizia di aggressione
capace di destare dolore.
Finché, nel tempo del piacere,
non si ricrea la capacità di soffrire,
manca la sensibilità al dolore.
Mentre quelli che sono sempre pronti a soffrire,
non hanno più l'esperienza del piacere,
lo cercano nel dolore,
ma allora non è partecipazione, compassione,
è attaccamento alla sofferenza, è dipendenza.
Così pensava il buon Nicola, così elargiva
giudizi sulla vita.

Portava in sé rigide determinazioni:
come quella di non credere

Nicola's spiteful severity noted
every flaw, he didn't forgive
weakness, uncertainty,
approximation, distraction.
Oh if he had seen them, instead, as indelible scars
of suffered blows,
if he had forgiven them or, even better, loved them
like war wounds, like inevitable signs
of inevitable crossings!

These scholars who use every conference
to make a show of expertise and ability!
And they demonstrate that they know and they make of knowledge
a discrimination between the intelligent and those who are not,
these scholars, when they are obliged to
go through the last door, how unprepared
they will show themselves to be!
Nicola couldn't tolerate the blissful smile
of those who, thanks to their intelligence, consider themselves ahead.

Once the reserve of compassion is spent,
there's no war, there's no disgrace,
there's no chilling news of aggression
capable of causing pain.
As long as in the time of pleasure,
the ability to suffer is not recreated,
the sensitivity to pain is missing.
While those who are always willing to suffer,
no longer have the experience of pleasure,
they seek it in pain,
but then it is not participation, compassion,
it is an attachment to suffering, it's a dependency.
This was good Nicola's thinking, how he proffered
judgments on life.

He carried within himself harsh determinations:
like that of believing

che ai rapporti individuali,
o l'altra, la decisione presa un bel giorno
di non contraddire più gli interlocutori.
Ricordava l'episodio. Il suo fedele amico
Alfonso Mieli si era infervorato in una distinzione:
tra il romanzo dell'Ottocento che – diceva –
crea un mondo, e in questo slancio inventivo
sta il suo irresistibile fascino e valore,
e il romanzo attuale, che si preoccupa del tema,
di trovare un tema coinvolgente e morboso,
coinvolgente perché morboso, morboso
perché nutrito di scrittura esibizionistica,
scrittura che promette di mostrare l'intimità.
Nicola aveva imparato che non contraddire
dava spazio a un'esperienza più ampia,
a un pensiero più libero.
Alfonso si era meravigliato di quel silenzio.

Se l'uomo vede una verità che gli altri non vedono,
è vanità, è atto vanitoso e vano?
Può un mortale comprendere ciò che gli altri mortali
non comprendono, e attingere alla verità?
Possono le costruzioni del pensiero e le parole umane
rivelare una verità superiore alle parole, al pensiero?
Può un'impeccabile costruzione logica garantire
se stessa come assoluta verità?
Solo la fede può garantire che le parole
rivelino la verità, siano la verità –
la filosofia non può che fare
continuo ricorso alla fede -,
come accade per ogni affermazione,
anche per questa.

only in individual relations,
or the other, the decision taken one fine day
to no longer contradict his interlocutors.
He recalled the incident. His faithful friend
Alfonso Mieli was all excited about a distinction
between the nineteenth-century novel which – he said –
creates a world, and in this inventive leap
lies its irresistible appeal and value,
and today's novel, which is concerned with the theme,
of finding a theme that is engrossing and morbid,
engrossing because it is morbid, morbid
because it's nourished by pretentious writing,
writing that promises to reveal intimacy.
Nicola had learned that not contradicting
gave space to a more ample experience,
to freer thought.
Alfonso was amazed by that silence.

If man sees a truth that others do not,
is it useless, is it a futile and pointless act?
Can a mortal comprehend that which other mortals
do not, and tap the truth?
Can the constructions of thought and human words
reveal a higher truth than words, than thought?
Can an impeccable, logical construction guarantee
itself as an absolute truth?
Only faith can guarantee that words
reveal the truth, are truth –
philosophy can only make
continuous reference to faith -,
as happens with every affirmation,
even for this one.

Si può pensare che esista un Essere indipendente
dal pensiero umano? Vi si può credere.
Si può pensare che l'Essere, come l'universo,
abbia preceduto la presenza umana?
Dicono che si può dimostrare, ma è meglio dire
che vi si può credere.
Si può pensare che l'Essere sia ciò che l'uomo
riesce a leggerne, a capirne?
Oppure che sia Altro rispetto alla capacità
di comprensione umana?
Certo, vi si può credere e vi si può non credere.
Così la teoresi non è forse una
delle più pure creazioni dell'intelletto umano?

Non si può sapere – pensava Alfonso –
come sarebbe il mondo se gli uomini
amassero Dio, lo seguissero
con tutto il cuore, ascoltassero
le sue prescrizioni e i precetti: si può immaginare
che non ci sarebbero più intemperie,
terremoti, alluvioni, siccità,
e nemmeno più malattie e paure.
Vi si può credere.

Can it be imagined that a Being exists independent
of human thought? One might believe this.
Can it be imagined that this Being, like the universe,
preceded human existence?
They say this can be proven, but it's better to say
that one might believe this.
Can it be imagined that this Being is what man
is able to read into it, to understand about it?
Or that it is Something Else in relation to the ability
of human comprehension?
Of course, one might believe this and one may not.
So isn't speculation perhaps one
of the purest creations of human intellect?

We cannot know – thought Alfonso –
what the world would be like if men
loved God, followed him
with all their hearts, heeded
his advice and precepts: it can be imagined
that there would be no more severe weather,
earthquakes, floods, droughts,
and not even illnesses and fears.
One might believe this.

FABRIZIO SANI

Il muro del folletto

La primavera è finita in ritardo.
La luna è una scatola di fiammiferi
nella penombra di uno sgabuzzino,
molto, ma molto, affollato.
Tu sei più silenziosa del solito.
Io non ho abbastanza coraggio
perciò prendo a fumare il tuo silenzio.
Butto giù senza sputare nulla,
digerisco tutto:
silenzio,
luna,
primavera.
L'alfabeto occupa le linee telefoniche;
un bicchiere va in mille pezzi;
un folletto impasta il calcestruzzo.
Percorro l'ipotenusa di un triangolo rettangolo
per riaccompagnarti a casa.
Ci guardiamo un'ultima volta i piedi.
Ci guardiamo un'ultima volta gli stinchi.
Ci guardiamo un'ultima volta le ginocchia.
Ci guardiamo un'ultima volta il ventre.
Ci guardiamo un'ultima volta l'ombelico.
Ci guardiamo l'ultima volta il petto.
Il folletto si riposa un po' mentre il muro è già alto.
Ci guardiamo un'ultima volta il mento.
Ci guardiamo un'ultima volta la bocca e sospiro.
Ci guardiamo un'ultima volta il naso.
Ci guardiamo un'ultima volta gli occhi e i miei piangono.

The goblin's wall

Springtime has ended late.
The moon is a match box
in the twilight of a full,
extremely full, storage shed.
You are more quiet than usual.
I do not have enough courage
so I start smoking your silence
I gulp it down without spitting out
I digest everything:
silence.
moon,
springtime.
The alphabet takes over the telephone lines;
a glass shatters in a thousand pieces;
a goblin mixes the concrete.
I travel the hypotenuse of a right triangle
to accompany you back home.
We look at our feet one last time
We look at our shins one last time
We look at our knees one last time
We look at our bellies one last time
We look at our navels one last time
We look at our chests one last time.
The goblin takes a little rest as his wall is already high.
We look at our chins one last time
We look at our mouths one last time and I let out a sigh
We look at our noses one last time
We look each other in the eye one last time and mine are crying.

I tuoi sgridano il folletto che riprende.
Abbasso lo sguardo e ti vedo per l'ultima volta,
mentre il muro ti copre,
vorrei parlare ma ho assorbito troppo silenzio.
Non ci sarà mai più una parola.
Torno dove germoglia un fiore che mi consola
e gli racconto la storia
di un giovane ragazzo triste
che una volta è stato molto innamorato
e ha scoperto che non vuol dire felice.

Yours are scolding the goblin who is back at it.
I lower my gaze and I see you one last time,
as the wall hides you,
I would like to speak but I have absorbed too much silence.
Never will a word be spoken again.
I return to where a flower that consoles me sprouts
and I tell it the story
of a sad young boy
who was once very much in love
and discovered that it does not mean happiness.

Naupatia

Mio padre aveva scarpe spesse,
diceva buone per passeggiare.
In tasca una castagna e un coltello che funziona,
perfetto;
servivano entrambi per non ammalarsi.
Lui si fingeva adulto
e io fingevo di crederci:
solo nella finzione
è potuto sopravvivere un dialogo di affetto.
Mi ha sempre guardato come un battello
attraverso il quale esplorare il mare,
sudava freddo ai miei spostamenti attorno
alla staticità dei suoi occhi,
perdeva l'equilibrio al mio oscillare,
e tutta quella ricerca di una trasandata libertà
si è consumata sui miei argini
in un indefinito malessere
negoziato con le sue fragilità,
le sue bugie che sono le mie.

Seasickness

My father had thick shoes,
he used to say they were good for walking.
In his pocket, a chestnut and a working knife,
perfect;
they both kept one from falling ill.
He pretended to be an adult,
and I pretended to believe that:
only through pretense
could a dialog of affection survive.
He always saw me as a boat
through which to explore the sea,
he'd break out in cold sweats at my moving around
the immobility of his eyes,
at my wavering, he would lose balance
and all that searching for a lazy freedom,
was worn down at my defenses
into a indefinite uneasiness
bargained with his fragility,
his lies that are my own.

Veduta di campagna con bar

Le macchine passano a velocità diverse davanti al bar,
io riconosco le persone che le guidano.
L'aria assume le tinte gialle del neon.
È uno stato emotivo cui non riesco ad adattarmi.
Il Bianchi viene a prendere mezzo chilo di pane bucato
e la pagnotta per Agata alle dieci in punto,
Flavio e il Cioni fanno avanti e indietro in continuazione
per Campari e birra "ghiacciata, mi raccomando".
Vittorio finisce di pranzare prima di mezzogiorno
e viene a prendere caffè e Futura e poi chiede:
"ancora non c'è Bronzino?", e così via.
Ronzano nel sottofondo i frigoriferi,
tintinna il perno arrugginito della ventola,
dalla cucina s'incuneano timbri metallici e aroma unto.
Come affacciato a un fiume, osservo fluire
le battute riciclate di bar in bar dai clienti.
Con cadenza regolare viene urlato il mio nome
e mi riacciuffa quest'assurda dimensione.
La mia giornata è impressa nel solco della sedia.
Il giorno s'inabissa nella notte e riemerge identico.
Dio è qui che ha appiccicato la sua gomma da masticare.
Vorrei che accadesse qualcosa, anche la più tragica,
per soddisfare la mia nevrastenia e far cedere
il chiodo che sorregge questo quadro intollerabile.
Penso a Bucarest, a un fratello che ci abita:
è un'ora più vicino alla notte e ai sogni,
all'evasione precaria dalla contingenza.

View of countryside with bar

Cars pass at different speeds in front of the bar,
I recognize the people driving them.
The air takes on the yellow tints of the neon light.
It is an emotional state to which I cannot adapt..
At ten on the dot, Bianchi comes to grab a pound of the bread with holes
and the daily loaf for Agata,
Flavio and Cioni go back and forth continuously
for Campari and beer, " make sure it's ice cold."
Vittorio finishes lunch before noon
and comes by to get coffee and cigarettes and then asks:
"still no Bronzino?", and so it goes.
The refrigerators hum in the background,
the rusted pivot of the fan clinks,
from the kitchen filter in metallic notes and greasy aroma.
As if facing a river, I observe the flow
of jokes recycled by customers from bar to bar.
With regular rhythm, my name is shouted
and this absurd dimension captures me.
My day is imprinted on the groove of the chair.
The day sinks into night and re-emerges identical.
God is here, where he has stuck his chewing gum.
I wish something would happen, even the most tragic of things,
to satisfy my nervous exhaustion and remove
the nail that holds up this intolerable picture.
I think of Bucharest, of a brother who lives there;
one hour closer to nighttime and to dreams,
to the precarious escape from the circumstances.

Parco d'inverno

Mi ricordo un parco d'inverno.
L'erba umida.
L'ordine complesso con cui il vento
riordinava il ciarpame,
i sentimenti,
riportandoli nei corpi da dove erano sfuggiti.
Mi ricordo le sei di pomeriggio in un parco d'inverno.
La tenerezza sfilacciata di una coppia,
su una panchina trascina un abbraccio oltre il buio.
Mi ricordo una grossa nuvola grigia che correva via velocissima
da quel parco d'inverno
e un corvo nero che a un certo punto ci sparì dentro.
Mi ricordo una lacrima cadere in un parco d'inverno,
con il buio
e l'erba già umida
nessuno ci ha fatto caso.
Il gelsomino, dicono,
è un fiore che ritorna.

A park in winter

I remember a park in winter.
The wet grass.
The complex order in which the wind
was rearranging the rubbish,
the emotions,
carrying them back to the bodies they escaped from.
I remember six o'clock in the evening in a park in winter.
The frayed tenderness of a couple
on a park bench
carries their embrace beyond the dark.
I remember a large grey cloud that was rushing by, fast
from that park in winter
and a black crow which, at a certain point, disappeared inside of it.
I remember a tear falling in a park in winter,
with the darkness
and the already wet grass
nobody noticed it
Jasmine, they say, is a flower that comes back.

DONATELLA DELLA RATTA

L'immagine sparita

Parte I

Voce:
Bassel è un *geek*.
Ci incontriamo un giorno, per caso, al caffè zerounozero.

Io sono in chat, lui pure.

Siamo uno di fronte all'altra, soli con i nostri computer.

Un amico americano ci ha e-presentato ma noi però ci i-ncontriamo schermo a schermo nel caffè zerounozero, per caso.

Bassel è un *geek*, non parla ma fa magie al computer.
Se gli prende bene fa battute. Parla di sesso, impreca.

La casa di Bassel è il computer, lui capisce solo quel mondo.
Una volta è andato in Cina, per due settimane.
Gli ho chiesto: raccontami com'è la Cina.
Ha detto, e che ne so, ho visto solo il computer, e qualche puttana. Scopano bene però...

(pausa)

Andiamo in giro per geek fest, barcamp, twestival, tech meetings, net conferences, unconferences, PechaKucha.
Postiamo, tagghiamo, twittiamo, uplodiamo, ci spariamo ore interminabili di Internet zerounozero.

The Vanished Image

Part I

Voice:
Bassel is a *geek*.
We meet one day, by chance at the zeroonezero café.

I am in a chatroom, so is he.

We sit in front of each other, alone with our computers.

An American friend has e-introduced us but we e-meet screen to screen in the zeroonezero café by chance.

Bassel is a *geek*, he doesn't speak but performs magic on the computer.
If he's in the mood he jokes. Talks about sex, swears.

Bassel's home is the computer, he only understands that world.
Once he went to China for two weeks.
I said: tell me about China.
He said: what do you want to know? I only saw the computer, and some whores. But they fuck well...

(pause)

We go to geek fests, barcamps, twestival, tech meetings, net conferences, unconferences, PechaKuchas.
We post/ tag/ tweet /upload/pass endless hours on the Internet zeroonezero.

Io e Bassel siamo sempre insieme. Lui mi ha installato Ubuntu e iniziato all'open source.

Va di moda la parola "blogger arabo". Il New York Times ci fa gli articoli. Repubblica ci fa gli articoli...."La blogger araba velata"...

Lo porto a un meeting di "blogger arabi" e Bassel dice: ma che cazzo fanno questi? il blogger o lo fai sul serio oppure meglio vendere patate...ti pare che possiamo seriamente parlare di politica qui, in questo buco di culo di Medioriente?

(pausa)

Un anno solo passa, e Bassel é lui l'idolo dei "blogger arabi". Non vive più dentro il suo computer, ma in una schifosa prigione nella periferia di Damasco, dove per trovarlo sua moglie deve attraversare il fuoco incrociato, regime, ribelli, ribelli, regime, ribelli, esercito libero, Nusra, ISIS, ISIL, figli del profeta, figli liberi del profeta, profeta libero dei figli, profeta liberato dai figli, figli liberi ma non liberati, figli liberati ma non liberi...

Bassel è un bit zerounozero. È l'hashtag di se stesso. La sua faccia è su tutti i giornali, su tutti i siti del mondo, su tutti gli schermi del sistema solare...

poveri piccoli siriani, calpestati, violati, violentati, aperti a metà, ingoiati a bocconi dal mondo intero.
Poveri-poveri-poveri
piccoli- piccoli-piccoli pixel di sangue 24frame al secondo divorati su smartphone e tablet, refreshati a manetta per non perdere l'alta definizione dell'orrore

(pausa)

Il sapere è il bene supremo.
Io so, tu sai. Io faccio, tu fai.
Tu non sai, perciò non fai.
Io voglio che tu sappia, così farai.

Bassel and I are always together. He installed Ubuntu for me and initiated me into open source.

The word "Arab blogger" is fashionable. The New York Times writes articles on them. Repubblica does too, better if a woman: "The veiled Arab blogger"...

I bring him to a meeting of "Arab bloggers" and Bassel says: what the fuck are these people? If you're a blogger do it seriously or better to sell potatoes... you think you can seriously talk about politics here, in this fuck damn Middle East?

(pause)

A year later, and Bassel is the idol of "Arab bloggers". He no longer lives inside his computer, but in a filthy prison in the suburbs of Damascus. If his wife wants to visit him, she has to walk through the crossfire, the regime, the rebels, other rebels, regime, rebels, free army, Nusra, ISIS, ISIL, sons of the prophet, free sons of the prophet, prophet of free sons, prophet freed from sons, free but not liberated sons of the prophet, liberated but not free sons...

Bassel is a zeroonezero bit. He is the #hashtag of himself. His face is in all the newspapers, on all the world's sites, on all the screens in the solar system...

poor little Syrians, trampled, violated, raped, cut open, swallowed by the mouthful by the whole world.
Poor-poor-poor things
small-small-small pixels of blood 24 frames per second devoured on smartphones and tablets, constantly refreshed so as not to lose the high definition of horror

(pause)

Knowledge is the greatest asset.
I know, you know.
I do, you do.
You do not know, so you do not do.
I want you to know, so you will do.

Sono passati sei anni e....
duemilioniquattrocentomilacinquecentoventidue video
diecimilionicinquecentoquarantatrevirgolazerozerozero hashtag
un milardoeventimilatrecentomiliardidimilioni *di like, share*

Il mondo sa.
Il mondo non fa.
Il mondo condivide zerounounozerozerounounozerouno.

Anche tu Bassel, adesso, sei un bit zerounozerounozerounozero che viaggia alla velocità della luce da Bejing a Silicon Valley in Norvegia a Berlino nelle aule delle università nei cool gathering nelle mobilitazioni di lotta per i diritti umani nelle piazze nei centri sociali nelle tivù nei premi internazionali...

Puoi viaggiare senza passaporto, fregartene, riprodurti, copiarti e incollarti, condividerti, taggarti, uplodarti, diventare l'avatar di te stesso...

..hai finalmente la tua libertà, Bassel, la libertà zerounozero.

Parte II

Voce 1: L'immagine è un atto e non una cosa, dice Sartre.

Voce 2: A tratti, l'immagine non si ha voglia di vederla, dice Godard.
L'immagine è difficile.

Voce 1: Filmare ad ogni costo. Filmare per informare. Filmare per vedere e farsi vedere.
L'immagine è difficile, è proprio vero, Jean Luc.

(pausa)

Voce 2: Resisti, piccolo siriano, resisti, e filma per noi.

Six years have passed by....
Two million, four hundred thousand, five hundred and twenty two videos
Ten million five hundred and forty three zero zero zero hashtags
One billion and twenty thousand three hundred billion million likes, shares

The world knows.
The world does nothing.
The world shares zerooneonezerozeroneonezeroone.

You too Bassel, now, you are a bit zeroonezeroonzeroonzeroone that travels at the speed of light from Beijing to Silicon Valley, from Norway to Berlin in the classrooms of universities in cool gatherings in the fights for human rights in squares in the social centers in TVs in international prizes...

You can travel without a passport, not giving a shit, reproduce yourself, copy and paste yourself, share yourself, tag yourself, upload yourself, become the avatar of yourself...

...you finally have your freedom, Bassel: the freedom zeroonezeroone.

Part II

Voice 1: The image is an act and not a thing, Sartre says.

Voice 2: Sometimes you don't want to see the image, Godard says.
The image is difficult.

Voice 1: Film at any cost. Film to inform. Film to see and to be seen.
The image is difficult, it's true, Jean Luc.

(pause)

Voice 2: Resist, little Syrian, resist, and film for us.

Voce 1:
...una guerriglia di centinaia di migliaia di telefonini...la nostra grande rivoluzione pixel.

Voce 2:
Signora della camera, prega per noi.

Voce 1:
(un calcio in bocca alla bella bocca fine del piccolo siriano che filma, sangue da tutte le parti,
"sei tu cane quello che ha girato quella roba? Ti ho visto non mi dire cazzate. Il Tubeschermo sa tutto, vede tutto.
Calci. Sangue. Denti che volano.
Ed ora passiamo all'elettricità...)

Voce 2:
Signora della camera, prega per noi.

Voce 1:
Tutto il popolo siriano filma: filmano i giovani che manifestano per le strade...

Voce 2:
(questo si che è uno smartphone, megapixel con le contropalle per afferrarla tutta la libertà)

Voce 1:
...filmano i torturatori nelle carceri

Voce 2:
(milioni, centinaia di milioni di clip invadono i Tubeschermi del mondo intero. Primo piano, fuori fuoco, fuori campo, campo lungo, inquadratura a destra, inquadratura a sinistra, close up, long shot, plan sequence)

Voice 1:
...guerrilla warfare by hundreds of thousands of mobile phones... our great pixelated revolution..

Voice 2:
Our Lady of the camera, pray for us.

Voice 1:
(a kick in the mouth, of the beautiful mouth of the little Syrian who films, blood on all sides,
"Are you the one who shot that stuff? I saw you, don't give me that bullshit."
The Tubescreen knows everything, sees everything.
Kicks. Blood. Flying teeth.
And now let's move on to electricity...)

Voice 2:
Lady of the camera, pray for us.

Voice 1:
The whole of the Syrian people film: the young people demonstrating on the streets film...

Voice 2:
This is a smartphone, megapixel and wow! to grab all the freedom!

Voice 1:
....they film torturers in prisons...

Voice 2:
(millions, hundreds of millions of clips invade the Tubescreens of the entire world.
Foreground, middleground, background, out of focus, reverse angle, point of view shot, high-angle shot, low-angle shot, close-up, one shot, long take)

Voce 1:
... filmano i ribelli armati e filmano i militari del dittatore.

(pausa)

Voce 2:
..e non è solo che un film oggi può farsi di queste immagini altrui, perché non esiste immagine altrui

Voce 1:
(filmiamo, trasferiamo, uplodiamo, condividiamo..
condividiamo, uplodiamo, trasferiamo, filmiamo.
Le notti, i giorni, i giorni, le notti)

Voce 2:
Dimmelo tu Bassel...
take one: primo martire,
take two: secondo martire,
take milioni di milioni di milioni di
martiri.

(pausa)

Voce 1:
Cerco l'immagine.
Cammino per le strade, volo per le strade inseguendo l'immagine.
La cerco in quelle facce, mi chiedo vi chiedo perché, perché siete qui?

Voce 2:
Lui non cerca l'immagine, lui fa l'immagine...
..indomabile, indistruttibile, schizzata come il fulmine.

Voce 1:
La fermo, la guardo, la ammiro...
La corsa in picchiata per fare l'immagine,

Voice 1:
...They film the armed rebels, they film the dictator's soldiers.

(Pause)

Voice 2:
..and it's not just that today a film can be made of other people's images, because *there is no image of other people.*

Voice 1:
(we film, we transfer, we upload, we share ..
we share, we upload, we transfer, we film.
The nights, the days, the days, the nights)

Voice 2:
Tell me, Bassel...
take one: first martyr,
take two: second martyr,
take millions of millions of
martyrs.

(pause)

Voice 1:
I'm looking for the image.
I walk the streets, fly in the streets, chasing the image.
I look for it in those faces, I ask myself why, I ask you why, why are you here?

Voice 2:
He doesn't look for the image, he makes the image...
...invincible, unbreakable, flashing like lightning.

Voice 1:
I stop, I look at her, I admire her...
Swooping down to make the image,

la corsa di quelli come Bassel che hanno corso per prendervi, per catturarvi....

Voce 2: ...dannate maledette maledettissime immagini!

Voce 1: ...c'è ancora, un residuo è rimasto, si è incagliato fra i pixel della morte e dice:

(pausa)

Voce 2: io sono la corsa prima della morte, io c'ero, io ci sono.

Voce 1: ...la corsa prima della morte, la corsa prima che la vita diventasse morte... la corsa.

Voce 2: Signora della camera, prega per noi.

Omaggio a Bassel Khartabil Safadi (1981-2015), giustiziato dal regime siriano per aver filmato la libertà, e ai migliaia di giovani siriani morti, come lui, per l'Immagine.

the race of those like Bassel who ran to catch you, to capture you....

Voice 2: ...damned, cursed, infernal images!

Voice 1: ...there is some left, there's a residue, it is stranded among the pixels of death and says:

(pause)

Voice 2: I am the race before death, I was there, I am there.

Voice 1: ...the race before death, the race before life becomes death... the race...

Voice 2: Lady of the camera, pray for us.

For Bassel Khartabil Safadi (1981-2015), put to death by the Syrian regime for having filmed freedom and for the thousands of young Syrians who like him died for the Image.

JONIDA PRIFTI

La Portatrice Carnica

Disturbo dal ricordo
allargata raggiera
così, in sosta dal senso di dire
in quale forma sono?

Una testa di chiodo
orma, attorno l'ultima ferita
un pezzo di polmone
ridurre, dal peso in diffusione

per mezzo di voci si ripercuote
dalle fonti di collo
m'arriva l'urlo
alla sua sonnolenza improvvisa

nebbia, dal fondovalle
detrito di un sole
eclisse indolente, prosciugarsi
in alba persa, allungo confini

sprofondarsi, dentro strati di neve
innevato tronco in zona di *zèi*[1]
detergo fronti caldi
guardiana d'un tratto in disuso

bianca - nera sembianza
volutamente estratta, dal tempo
non trae vigore se
tritata è la forma

sovrastante persona al vertice
vengo astratta dalla vita in giù
in vortice l'urto
del bulbo oculare

---

[1] Gerle (dialetto friulano)

The Carnic Bearer

Disturbance from
the memory
widened halo
what shape am I in?

The head of a nail
trace, around the last wound
a piece of lung
reduce, from the weight in diffusion

by means of voices struck again
from the sources of neck
I receive the scream
To her sudden sleepiness

fog, from the valley bottom
detritus of a sun
indolent eclipse, dry up
in lost dawn, I lengthen borders

collapse, in layers of snow
snow-covered trunk in the area of *zèi*[2]
I cleanse scorching fronts
guardian of a move in disuse

white - black appearance
intentionally extracted, from time
it doesn't derive vigor if
the form is ground

looming person at the vertex
I become abstracted from the waist down
in vortex the impact
of the eyeball

---

[1] 'Baskets' in Friulian dialect.

ghirlanda colossale
orli, crespi d'altura figura
in quale verso il tiro penetra?

Corpo da tale alcova abbonda.

Semicerchio addentra percorrenza
miraggio di alcuna consistenza
sottile timbro d'orecchio sale
curvilineo cratere in carne

polla del gentil sesso
fessura d'insorgenza
quanto la vena stessa

non solo latitudine reale
dislocato sangue d'era vitale
rimbombo remoto dal bassopiano
giunge dritto al cranio

discendere dal centro dell'addome
deglutire l'intero raggio d'ombra
escoriarsi da indietro le spalle
per quanto tempo sei via?

Dall'antro uterino, bomba d'acqua
diurno stagno d'uccelli, a ridosso
gira elmo del fare

nel vento di maestro, all'inverso
d'altopiano, squarciare il valico
maciullarsi, di croste modellate
di falde in rilievo
sondare versanti di immagini

stillare in filari di anelli
entro fluidi d'alberi intimi
con elevato stupore, librare

colossal wreath
hems, crinkled of prominent figure
in which direction does the shot penetrate?

Body from such alcove abounds.

Semicircle enters instance
mirage of some consistency
subtle timbre of ear rises
curvilinear crater in flesh

wellspring of the fair sex
fissure of insurgence
as much as the vein itself

not simply real latitude
dislocated blood of vital era
remote rumble from the lowland
arrives straight to the cranium

descend from the center of the abdomen
swallow the entire ray of shadow
excoriate itself from behind the shoulders
how long are you away?

From the uterine antrum, daytime
downpour pond of birds, nearby
lurks the helmet of action

in the northwest wind, the reverse
of the plateau, rip open the strata
mangle, of crusts modelled
on strata in relief
probe slopes of images

exude in rows of rings
within fluids of intimate trees
with heightened amazement, balance

quale proiezione residua del se?

Materia di mille corpi idrici
recettore della parte depressa
del transire tra sezione areica
di anime portate per deflusso

a ritornare, da distanti solchi
vibrare per canto sorde vocali

cippo in là, limiti
via sonante fluviale

di resti confinari, le carniche
a disseminare, grammi di pelli
per flusso ematico, invocano

catene calcaree, vette in su
roccia compatta, fiori a contatto
pensiero circolare
con la morsa sul piede
verticale passo, di vita breve

fiocco lento lento, pura radiosa
sacerdotessa, vestale erboso
dal monte Peralba, traina l'ululo
per il campo rosso, ripido pendio
percuote da torrenti rovesciati
a sciogliere la breve tua comparsa

dalle rive opposte sotto asse
sdentati passaggi di lampo per due
sottratto fondo storto
nel sogno, la grotta pare cartone

se ad avanzare possiamo in tre
muscolo triangolare
attecchire labbra insieme secche

which residual projection of oneself?

Material of a thousand hydric bodies
receptor of the depressed part
of passing through between areal section
of souls carried as outflow

to return, from distant furrows
vibrate in song deaf vowels

milestone over there, limits
by way of resounding fluvial

scattering, grams of skins
by way of hematic flow,
they invoke

limestone chains, peaks above
compact rock, flowers in contact
circular thought
with the vise on its vertical
foot pass, of short life

steady steady flake, pure radiant
priestess, grassy vestal
from mount Peralba, tows the howl
throughout the red field, steep slope
strikes by overturned torrents
to dissolve your brief existence

from the opposite shores under plank
toothless landscapes of lightning for two
removed crooked bottom
in the dream, the grotto resembles cardboard

if to move forward we can in three
triangular muscle
press lips together dry

di solitarie lingue in sospeso

tra denti neri duole
l'idea del domani notturno
quale sostanza a riempir potrebbe?

(Agosto 2019)

Nota

Estratto dal poema "La Portatrice Carnica". Il poema è ispirato alla figura di Maria Plozner Mentil, la quale durante la prima guerra mondiale operava, lungo il fronte della Carnia, insieme ad altre donne, trasportando con la sua gerla rifornimenti e munizioni fino alle prime linee italiane. Le donne che facevano questo lavoro venivano chiamate "Le portatrici carniche". L'unica a morire fu proprio Maria, a soli 32 anni, sotto il tiro mortale di un cecchino austriaco, il 15 febbraio del 1916, a quota 1619 di Casera Malpasso, nel settore Alto But. Al momento della morte vigeva su di lei la sua compagna di viaggio Rosalia Primus Bellina. Il poema è liberamente ispirato all'ultimo giorno di vita di Maria.

of solitary tongues suspended

between black teeth aches
the thought of nocturnal tomorrow
what substance could it fill?

(August 2019)

Note

Taken from the poem "The Carnic Bearer." The inspiration for the poem is Maria Plozner Mentil, who, with other women during WWI, transported supplies and munitions in baskets along the Carnia front; that is, up to the front lines in northeastern Italy. The women who carried out this work were referred to as the "Carnic bearers" (or "Carnic Messengers"). The only woman who died was Maria, aged 32, fatally shot by an Austrian sharpshooter on February 15, 1916 at Casera Malpasso, in the Alto But sector at 1,619 meters above sea level. As she died, her travel companion Rosalia Primus Bellina watched over her. The poem is freely inspired by Maria's last day of life.

Liri SM

a Daniele

Arrivi nel sogno per dire delle figure erette
di legno, in boschi fitti, dice il guardiano
del tuo ritorno *nga pylli*[3]
un passaggio di merli tira ossute ossa in sé
dentro le scie del treno s'inonda la partita.

Le voci diventano echi di fumo
dopo l'artificio del rogo
la gola mira al dunque.

Dea del solstizio come uno strazio
stai sul bordo della tua stessa bocca.

Nei colli del suono
affonda, al richiamo del cane
dal naso tornante
in tubi violacei, ritorna
sul vitreo stabile
non dalla ruota di fuoco
sotto il trono, mastica cenere.

Cosa pensa Daniele con l'AK-47?

Caduta la testa, dal tavolo di ciliegio
sopra le ciglia, dall'alto.

---

[3] Dall'albanese "dal bosco"

Liri SM (Free SM)

for Daniele

You arrive in a dream to speak of erect wooden
beings, in thick forests, the guardian says
of your return *nga pylli*[4]
a passing of sparrows pulls angular bones into itself
within the wakes of the train the departure is flooded.

Voices become echoes of smoke
after the artifice of the blaze
the gorge gazes at the result.

Goddess of the solstice like a torment
you are on the edge of your own mouth.

In the hills of the sound
it sinks, at the dog's call
from the hairpin nose
in violaceous tubes, it returns
on the glassy stable
not from the wheel of fire
beneath the throne, it chews ash.

What does Daniele think with his AK-47?

Head fallen, from the cherrywood table
above the eyelashes, from on high.

---

[4] "From the forest" in Albanian.

Neverending

Di notte assale la testa
un movimento dal tetto
a scricchiolare, nel silenzio delle travi
fionda la mano, caccia al centro nervoso
funicolo di acqua marina s'impregna del fossile.

Fanali al lato opposto, a evocare finali
al lento dilatare dei cunicoli nella saliva
finestra, dove guardare a testa in giù.

(Giugno 2019)

Neverending

At night a movement
from the roof assails the head,
creaking, in the silence of the beams
the hand hurls, hunt for the nerve center
funicle of seawater is sodden with the fossil.

Headlights on the opposite side, evoking finales
in the slow dilation of the burrows in the saliva
window, where you gaze upside down.

(June 2019)

POETS' BIOGRAPHIES

VINCENZO BAGNOLI
He is one of the founders of the literary magazine *Versodove*. He has published the collections: *33 giri stereo LP* (Gallo & Calzati, Bologna 2004), *FM - Onde corte* (Bohumil, Bologna 2007), *Deep Sky* (d'if, Naples, 2008), *Offscapes. Beyond the Limits of Urban Landscapes* (Trafika Europe, New York, 2016); Italian edition: *Offscapes. La parte distante del paesaggio – The distant part of the landscape* (Sala Editori, Pescara, 2017*); Soundscapes. 33 giri Extended Play* (Carteggi letterari, Messina, 2018).

CARLO BOASSA
Born in Cagliari, he lives in Pistoia. After earning a doctorate in Comparative Literature, he worked as an editor. He has published the poetry collections *Un quaderno* (Longo, Ravenna, 1989) and *Autovita* (Longo, Ravenna, 1990) both finalists of the Dessì Prize, and the sylloge *Gli occhi* (Astra Editrice, Quartu S. Elena, Cagliari, 1993).

CHANDRA LIVIA CANDIANI
She was born in Milan. She has published: *Io con vestito leggero* (Campanotto, Udine, 2005);
La nave di nebbia. Ninnananne per il mondo (La biblioteca di Vivarium, Milan, 2005); *Bevendo il tè con i morti* (Interlinea, Novara, 2015); *La bambina pugile ovvero la precisione dell'amore* (Einaudi Turin, 2014 – Camaiore Prize 2014); *Ma dove sono le parole?* (Poems written by the children of the multiethnic suburbs of Milan during workshops held by Candiani, (co-edited with A. Cirolla, Effigie Edizioni, Pavia, 2015); *Fatti vivo* (Einaudi, Turin, 2017); *Il silenzio è cosa viva. L'arte della meditazione* (Einaudi, Turin, 2018); *Vista dalla luna* (Salani, Milan, 2019); *La domanda della sete 2016-2020* (Einaudi, Turin, 2020).

GIANNI D'ELIA
He founded and directed the magazine "Lengua" (1982-1994), born thanks to the relationship with Roberto Roversi. He has collaborated as a critic with numerous magazines and newspapers and his essays have been published *in Il Manifesto, Poesia, Nuovi Argomenti,* and *L'Unità*. He has published various poetry collections including: *Notte privata* (Einaudi, Turin,1993); *Congedo della vecchia Olivetti* (Einaudi, Turin, 1996), translated and published in France in 2005 by Bernard Simeone; *Bassa stagione* (Einaudi, Turin, 2003). In 2005 he published *L'eresia di Pasolini. L'avanguardia della tradizione dopo Leopardi* (Effigie, Milan, 2005). In 1993 he won the Carducci prize and in 2007 - together with Antonio Pascale, Carlo Ginzburg, and Titos Patrikios - he was awarded

the Brancati Prize. In 1994 his poem "Memoria" was placed on a plaque in Pesaro in the square dedicated to Giovanni Falcone and Paolo Borsellino, in front of the Monument to the Resistance. He also wrote the lyrics of some songs for Claudio Lolli. His most recent poetry collections are *Fiori del mare* (Einaudi, Turin 2015) and *Il suon di lei* (Luca Sossella Editore, Rome, 2020).

DONATELLA DELLA RATTA
She is a scholar, writer, performer, and curator specializing in digital media and networked technologies, with a focus on the Arab world. She teaches Media and Communications at John Cabot University in Rome. She has curated several international art exhibitions and film programs, including "Syria off frame," a collective show of 140 Syrian artists in collaboration with Luciano Benetton's Imago Mundi (Fondazione Cini, Venice, 2015), and "Syrian New Waves" on contemporary image-making in Syria (The Eye Film Museum, Amsterdam, 2017). In 2020 she co-curated the Read My World literary festival in Amsterdam, where she was also invited to read excerpts from *Stazione degli occhi, o del corpo che si sottrae* (Kurumuny, Lecce, 2021) an upcoming book project in collaboration with Albanian poet Jonida Prifti.

FABIO DONALISIO
He was born in the province of Cuneo. He has published *miti logiche* (ExCogita, Milan, 2007), *la pratica del ritorno* (in *Poesia contemporanea. XI quaderno italiano,* Marcos y Marcos, Milan, 2012), *nulla più e nulla meno* (Isola, 2013, with drawings by Marco Corona), *ambienti saturi* (A27/Amos Edizioni, Venice, 2017), *il libro delle cose* (Aragno, Turin, 2018), and *la maraja* (with Nicola Peretti, self-published, 2020); *talkin the collateral damage jubilation blues* (in *Piccola antologia della peste*, Ronzani editore, Vicenza, 2020). He is editor of the literary pages of *Blowup* and is one of the founders of the publishing project *Nervi. Cammina.*

GINEVRA LILLI
She was born in Rome, where she lives and works. After her studies in the French language and three years in the United States, she completed her university studies in Communication and Journalism in Rome. Since childhood, she has taught herself both abstract drawing, and writing, which she combines with drawing. Adoptive daughter of the late writer, poet, and literary critic Laura Lilli, she became her curator of memory. She has exhibited in Rome and Milan and has published *Diario Ordinario* (Marco Saya Edizioni, Milan, 2014).

FRANCA MANCINELLI
She is the author of four books of poetry: *Mala kruna* (Manni, San Cesario, Lecce, 2007), *Pasta madre* (with an afterword by Milo De Angelis, Nino Aragno, Turin, 2013), *Libretto di transito* (Amos edizioni, Venice, 2018), *Tutti gli occhi che ho aperto* (Marcos y Marcos, Milan 2020). A selection of her poems is featured in the anthology *Nuovi poeti italiani 6*, edited by Giovanna Rosadini (Einaudi, Turin, 2012), and, with an introduction by Antonella Anedda, in

XIII Quaderno italiano di poesia contemporanea, edited by Franco Buffoni (Marcos y Marcos, Milan, 2017). Some of her texts have been translated into several foreign languages. The Bitter Oleander Press (Fayetteville, New York) has published *At an Hour's Sleep from Here: Poems* (2007-2019), and *The Little Book of Passage* (2018), translated by John Taylor.

NEFELI MISURACA
She taught at Yale University, where she received her Ph.D. in Literature and Art. In Cyprus, she taught art history and cultural studies at Frederick University. In Italy, she taught anthropology of art at Sapienza University of Rome, and she currently teaches literature and art courses at John Cabot, Temple University, and Loyola University. She has been an editor for films showcased in several international film festivals (Cannes, Berlin, Rotterdam). She has been art critic for *Cyprus Mail* and television critic for *Il Manifesto*. She is a translator as well as a poet and in 2017 she published the poetry collection *La Solitudine Maestosa* (La Vita Felice, Milan).

RENATA MORRESI
She is the author of four collections of poetry: *Terzo paesaggio* (Aragno, Turin, 2019); *Bagnanti* (Perrone, Rome, 2013; *La signora W.* (Camera verde, Rome, 2013); *Cuore comune* (peQuod, Ancona, 2010). Her poems and creative works have appeared in Italy and abroad, published in French, English and Spanish. In 2015 she received the "Premio Nazionale per la Traduzione" bestowed by the Italian Ministry of Culture for the translation of modern and postmodern poets (among whom: Emily Dickinson, Rachel Blau DuPlessis, Robert Lax, Annie Abrahams, and NourbeSe Philip). Morresi is one of the editors of the litblog *Nazione Indiana* <www.nazioneindiana.com> and she is the chief editor of the Lacustrine series for the small press Arcipelago Itaca Edizioni, <www.arcipelagoitaca.it>.

FABIO ORECCHINI
Poet, anthropologist, artist. He has published *Dismissione* (Luca Sossella Editore, Rome, 2014), *Per Os (*Sigismundus editrice, San Benedetto del Tronto 2016), and *Figura* (Oèdipus, Salerno, 2019). His works have appeared in numerous magazines including: *Alfabeta2, Versodove, L'Ulisse,* and *Nuovi Argomenti* and he is featured in the documentary *GenerazioneY – Poesia italiana ultima* produced by Rai5. He has performed site-specific installations in spaces such as the Ex G.I.L. in Campobasso (Molise), the Palazzetto dei Nobili in L'Aquila (Abruzzo), the Mole Vanvitelliana in Ancona (Marche), and in Rome at the National Library, the Hungarian Academy, the Argentina Theater and the Primoli Foundation. With the installation *TerraeMotus* he was awarded the 2018 "Elio Pagliarani" Prize. He collaborates with the magazine *Argo* and the publishing house Argolibri, for which he directs the "Talee" series. Also, he edited the first Italian edition of *After Lorca* by Jack Spicer (Gwynplaine/Argo, Ancona/Rome, 2018) and the volume *L'altra voce* (Giometti & Antonello, Macerata, 2019), a correspondence by the Argentine poet A. Pizarnik.

JONIDA PRIFTI
Poet, performer, and translator from Albanian to Italian and vice versa. Born in Berat, Albania, she emigrated to Rome in 2001. Among her publications: *Non voglio partorire...* (Alfabeta2, 2010); *Ajenk* (Transeuropa, Massa, 2011); *Patrizia Vicinelli. La poesia e l'azione* (Onyx, 2014); *Rivestrane* (Selva, 2017). In 2008, with Stefano Di Trapani she founded the sound poetry duo "Acchiappashpirt." Among her recordings: *Flutura* (UK, 2015); *Tola* (Canti Magnetici, 2017); *Strangerivers* (Filibusta Records, 2017); *Ge n e r a t A* (Upitup, UK, 2018). Since 2010, they have been organizing the annual Roman festival of sound poetry "Poesia Carnosa." www.jonidaprifti.com

FABRIZIO SANI
Born in the province of Arezzo in Tuscany, he lives in Rome, where he completed his undergraduate degree in Arts and Performing Sciences at Sapienza University. He is currently working on a master's degree in Publishing and Writing at the same university. He collaborates with Laura Ceccacci literary agency. He published his first book of poetry *Si innamoravano tutti di me e io del loro amore* in 2018 (Turin: SuiGeneris edition).

TIZIANO SCARPA
Born in Venice, he is a novelist, poet, and playwright. Scarpa's third novel, *Stabat Mater* (Serpent's Tail, London, 2011) was awarded the Strega Prize, Italy's most prestigious literary honor. His acclaimed *Venice is a Fish: a Sensual Guide* (Gotham Books, New York, 2008) is known throughout the world as an idiosyncratic celebration of Venice.

BEPPE SEBASTE
He is a poet, storyteller, and essayist. He has published many books, including: *L'ultimo buco nell'acqua* (with Giorgio Messori, Aelia Laelia, Reggio E., 1983); *Café Suisse e altri luoghi di sosta* (Feltrinelli, Milan, 1992); *Nessuno di questi mi appartiene* (Feltrinelli, Milan, 1994); *HP. L'ultimo autista di lady Diana (*Einaudi, Turin, 2007); *Fallire. Storia con fantasmi* (Independent production, Amazon, 2015); *Panchine. Come uscire dal mondo senza uscirne (*Laterza, Rome-Bari 2008, 6th ed., 2018), *Oggetti smarriti e altre apparizioni* (Laterza, Rome-Bari, 2009); *Come un cinghiale in una macchia d'inchiostro* (Aragno, Turin, 2018). In Narni (Umbria) he created La Stanza, a "place for the arts" and a residence for artists. www.beppesebaste.com

CESARE VIVIANI
Born in Siena in 1947, he lives in Milan. He has published the poetry books: *L'ostrabismo cara* (Feltrinelli, Milan, 1973); *Piumana* (Guanda, Milan, 1977); *L'amore delle parti* (Mondadori, Milan, 1981); *Summulae 1966-1972* (Scheiwiller, Milan,1983); *Merisi* (Mondadori, Milan, 1986); *Preghiera del nome* (Mondadori, Milan, 1990); *L'opera lasciata sola* (Mondadori, Milan, 1993); *Cori non io 1975-1977* (Crocetti, Milan, 1994); *Una comunità degli animi* (Mondadori, Milan, 1997); *Silenzio dell'universo* (Einaudi, Turin, 2000); *Passanti* (Mondadori, Milan,

2002). In 2003 Oscar Mondadori published an anthology of his poetic journey, Po*esie; La forma della vita* (Einaudi, Turin 2005); *Credere all'invisibile (*Einaudi, Turin, 2009); *Infinita fine* (Einaudi, Turin, 2012); *Osare dire* (Einaudi, Turin, 2016); *Ora tocca all'imperfetto* (Einaudi, Turin, 2020). He has also published books of aphorisms and literary essays, such as *La voce inimitabile* (il melangolo, Genoa, 2004); *Non date le parole ai porci* (il melangolo, Genoa, 2014); *La poesia è finita. Diamoci pace. A meno che...* (il melangolo, Genoa, 2018).

GIOVANNA CRISTINA VIVINETTO
Born in Syracuse, Sicily, she lives in Rome, where she earned a degree in Modern Philology at Sapienza University with a dissertation on the poetry of Franco Buffoni. *Dolore Minimo* (Interlinea, Novara, 2018) is her first book, and the first book of Italian poetry to address the subject of transsexuality. With an introduction by Dacia Maraini and an afterword by Alessandro Fo, the book was featured in Italy's major newspapers and won several prizes, including the Viareggio Opera Prima (2019) for best debut. *Dove non siamo stati* is Giovanna's second book of poems (Bur Rizzoli, Milan, 2020).

TRANSLATORS' BIOGRAPHIES

TOM BAILEY received his Ph.D. in Philosophy from the University of Warwick. After teaching at Warwick and the Open University, he moved to Italy, first as a researcher at the University of Pisa and now teaching at John Cabot University in Rome. His research focuses on ethics and political philosophy. At JCU he teaches courses in political philosophy, ethics and business ethics, introductory, modern and contemporary philosophy, the philosophy of art, the philosophy of love, and humanities research methods.

ANDREA CASSON teaches Italian language at the Fashion Institute of Technology in New York and translates from Italian to English. A firm believer in collaborative translation, Andrea has co- translated a range of diverse texts from the political essays by Antonio Negri to the satirical writings of Sara Vannelli. She greatly enjoys the challenge of translating poetry and is honored to be included in this edition of *InVerse*.

BERENICE COCCIOLILLO (see Editors' biographies)

ALLISON GRIMALDI DONAHUE teaches creative writing at John Cabot University. Her work has appeared in Electric Literature, The Brooklyn Rail, Words Without Borders, Flash Art, The Literary Review, BOMB, Tripwire, The Massachusetts Review, Prairie Schooner, and other places. Her book of poetry *Body to Mineral* was published by Publication Studio Vancouver in 2016. She is also co-author of *On Endings* (May 2019) with Delere Press. She is Associate Translation Editor at Anomaly Journal and active with the American Literary Translators' Association. She was recently an artist in residence at MAMbo, the Museum of Modern Art Bologna. Her translation of Carla Lonzi's *Self-portrait* is forthcoming in September 2021 from Divided Publishing, London.

SEAN MARK holds a Ph.D. in comparative literature and was 2018-19 Rome research fellow at the British School at Rome. He has published on Pound, Pasolini and Italian Futurism – including a recent essay in *The Edinburgh Companion to Ezra Pound and the Arts* – and his first monograph, *Pound and Pasolini: Poetics of Crisis*, is forthcoming with Palgrave Macmillan. His poems have appeared in *A Packet of Poems for Ezra Pound* (Clemson University Press, 2017), and he has edited and translated two books by contemporary Italian poets for Chelsea Editions Press (New York). He lives in Paris, where he teaches English at Cergy Paris Université.

JENNIFER PANEK is an associate professor of English at the University of Ottawa, where she specializes in English Renaissance drama. Her scholarly publications include a monograph on early modern English comedy, published by Cambridge University Press, and articles in journals such as *English Literary Renaissance*, *Renaissance Drama*, and *English Literary History*. Her translation of Danilo Balestra's historical novel *Tirati a Sorte* (English title *The Luck of the Draw*) was published in 2019 by Atene Edizioni.

GABRIELE POOLE is professor of English literature at University of Cassino, in southern Italy. Born in an American-Italian family in Naples, he grew up in Italy and in the United States. He holds a Ph.D. in English with a major in Critical Theory from the University of Notre Dame, as well as a Doctorate in Literature of English Speaking Countries from La Sapienza University in Rome. He is the author of essays on English and American theater, of a monographic study on the problem of arbitrariness in Ferdinand de Saussure, and of several translations of poetry from English into Italian and from Italian into English. In particular, he is the translator of a collection of poems by John Matthias and the author of an Italian verse translation of Byron's "The Giaour." He has translated numerous Italian poets for the international poetry website Poetry International (https://www.poetryinternational.org) and for the *InVerse: Italian Poets in Translation* series published by John Cabot University. He is currently working on an Italian poetic translation of *Everyman* with facing text.

RICCARDO PUGLIESE has a *Laurea in Lettere Moderne* degree from the University of Venice, Ca' Foscari and an M.A. in Classics from the University of Maryland. He recently published an article on freedom in existentialism, "Esistenzialismo e vertigine della libertà in Jean-Paul Sartre" in Studi Sartriani (2020).

ANDREW RUTT has taught English composition at John Cabot University since 2012. He has a B.A. in Fine Art and Critical Theory from Goldsmith's College, University of London and his M.A. thesis was about "Freedom and Redemption in the Sophoclean Narrative of Flannery O'Connor". He is the co-author of the university textbook, still in use in Rome 3, *The UK: Learning the Language, Studying the Culture*.

ELENA BUIA RUTT is a poet, translator and literary critic who holds degrees in Philosophy and Literature, and an MA in Journalism. As journalist, she contributes to cultural programs on Italian television and national newspapers. Elena's first book of poems (*Ti stringo la mano mentre dormi*, Fuorilinea) was published in 2012, while her second (*Il mio cuore è un asino*, Nottetempo) in 2015. Her next book of poems, *La sete*, will be published in September 2021. Elena and her husband Andrew Rutt are a translating duo and work collaboratively on texts from and into Italian and English, most recently translating poems by Rowan Williams and Mary Oliver, as well as Flannery O'Connor's *Prayer Journal* for Rizzoli. In addition, as collaborators with JCU's Italy Reads project, they have taught courses on Flannery O'Connor, Walt Whitman, and Rachel Carson to Italian high school teachers.

JAMES SCHWARTEN has translated into English Dacia Maraini's theatrical works, most notably *Extravagance and Three Other Plays* (John Cabot University Press, Rome, 2015). He has embraced various intellectual pursuits since receiving his Ph.D. in 2005. In 2014 he co-curated an exhibition on Nordic painters in the Abruzzo region of Italy at the turn of the 20th century (Rome's Gallery of Modern Art), and in 2019 he edited Vincenzo Patanè's monograph *The Sour Fruit: Lord Byron, Love & Sex*. He collaborates with *Guardian* correspondent in Italy Lorenzo Tondo, translating legal, scientific and economic texts from Italian to English, and is a regular translator and editor for publisher ICEIGeo studio editoriale in Milan. He is currently researching depopulation trends in rural Italy.

LAUREN SUNSTEIN was born in Philadelphia and earned degrees from Harvard and New York University. In 1989, in a conscious choice to live abroad, she settled in Rome as an English teacher and photographer. For decades, while teaching academic writing at John Cabot University, she has pursued a parallel career in translation. Specializing in art history and contemporary culture, she has translated books for prestigious art publishing houses in Italy, including Skira, Electa and Rizzoli, as well as catalogues for museums of the calibre of Scuderie del Quirinale, Ara Pacis, and Capodimonte. Her poetry translation was published in InVerse 2018.

KAY WALLACE was born in Britain many years ago, when it was still part of Europe. She lived in the north, then moved gradually south until she reached Hastings and ran out of land and moved abroad. She studied sociology at Newcastle and Kent Universities. She has called Egypt, Indonesia, France and several towns in Italy home. A variety of jobs, including radiographer, waitress, chambermaid, smuggler, English language teacher, director of a TEFL school, TV executive, news producer and editor have paid the rent. She now lives in Rome with her faithful dog George and works as a writer and translator of TV and movie scripts, and the occasional piece of poetry.

EDITORS' BIOGRAPHIES

BRUNELLA ANTOMARINI, Ph.D., teaches aesthetics and contemporary philosophy at John Cabot University in Rome. Among her publications: *Le macchine nubili* (Castelvecchi 2020); *Thinking Through Error* (Lexington Books, 2012); *The Maiden Machine* (Edge Books, 2013); "The Acoustical Pre-history of Poetry," in *New Literary History* (Vol.35, no.3, 2004). She has edited *Sulla traduzione* ("il cannocchiale", nn.1-2, 1996) and *Tradurre: travisare e vedere* ("il cannocchiale" no.1, 1998). She has translated books or sections of books by poets and writers such as Paul Vangelisti, Dino Garrone, and Margaret Avison. She co-edited with Paul Vangelisti the collection of poems by George Oppen, *Shipwreck of the Singular* (Modena 2018).

BERENICE COCCIOLILLO teaches Italian language and translation at John Cabot University, where she is also Director of Web Communications. She is one of the founders and organizers of the InVerse Poetry Festival. She has translated works by many Italian poets including Laura Accerboni, Antonella Anedda, Umberto Fiori, Andrea Gibellini, Jolanda Insana, Anna Cascella Luciani, Bianca Madeccia, Lidia Riviello, and Gian Mario Villalta. She often collaborates with translator Andrea Casson. Her most recent published translations appear in *Annelisa Alleva, Selected Poems* (Gradiva, New York, 2020, tr. G. Albano, B. Cocciolillo, J. Joseph, G. Lenhart, V. Melchioretto) and *Tommaso Binga: A Silenced Victory* (Mimosa House, London, 2019, tr. B. Cocciolillo, A. Casson, J. Benci, G. Poole).

ROSA FILARDI teaches Italian language and theater at John Cabot University. She is one of the founders and organizers of the *InVerse* poetry festival. She is an author of short stories and theatrical works. Some of her plays, co-authored with Monica Mioli, are collected in the book, *Vieni avanti che non ci son dei sassi*, (Pendragon, Bologna 2006). She was named a finalist for the Premio Fersen for dramaturgy, 4th edition 2008, with the monologue *Volo Verticale*, published by Editoria & Spettacolo (Rome, 2009). She is a professional (APID®) DanceTherapist and she has been collaborating with the Compagnia della Mia Misura, an integrated Dance-Theatre group, a project of social inclusion through art and dance.

© 2021 by John Cabot University Press
Via della Lungara 233, Roma 00165
© Copyright of unpublished works held by the individual poets

www.johncabot.edu